New Directions in Book History

Series Editors
Shafquat Towheed
Faculty of Arts
Open University
Milton Keynes, UK

Jonathan Rose
Department of History
Drew University
Madison, NJ, USA

As a vital field of scholarship, book history has now reached a stage of maturity where its early work can be reassessed and built upon. That is the goal of New Directions in Book History. This series will publish monographs in English that employ advanced methods and open up new frontiers in research, written by younger, mid-career, and senior scholars. Its scope is global, extending to the Western and non-Western worlds and to all historical periods from antiquity to the twenty-first century, including studies of script, print, and post-print cultures. New Directions in Book History, then, will be broadly inclusive but always in the vanguard. It will experiment with inventive methodologies, explore unexplored archives, debate overlooked issues, challenge prevailing theories, study neglected subjects, and demonstrate the relevance of book history to other academic fields. Every title in this series will address the evolution of the historiography of the book, and every one will point to new directions in book scholarship. New Directions in Book History will be published in three formats: single-author monographs; edited collections of essays in single or multiple volumes; and shorter works produced through Palgrave's e-book (EPUB2) 'Pivot' stream. Book proposals should emphasize the innovative aspects of the work, and should be sent to either of the two series editors.

More information about this series at
http://www.palgrave.com/gp/series/14749

Anna Kiernan

Writing Cultures and Literary Media

Publishing and Reception in the Digital Age

Anna Kiernan
University of Exeter
Streatham Campus, UK

ISSN 2634-6117   ISSN 2634-6125   (electronic)
New Directions in Book History
ISBN 978-3-030-75080-0   ISBN 978-3-030-75081-7   (eBook)
https://doi.org/10.1007/978-3-030-75081-7

Cover illustration: wujekjery / Getty Images

This Palgrave Pivot imprint is published by the registered company Springer Nature Switzerland AG.
The registered company address is: Gewerbestrasse 11, 6330 Cham, Switzerland

ACKNOWLEDGEMENTS

I feel very grateful to have worked with—and to continue to work with—such talented, creative people.

Thank you to my wonderful colleagues at Falmouth University and at the University of Exeter. I'm especially grateful for insights and support from Dr. Danielle Barrios O'Neill, Jon Cope, Dr. David Devanny, Dr. Niamh Downing, Dr. Abram Foley, Dr. Ruth Heholt, Dr. Amy Lilwall, Dr. Kym Martindale, Dr. Meredith Miller, Professor Jane Milling, Professor Heike Roms, Professor Linda Williams, Dr. Kate Wallis and Dr. Hannah Wood. Thank you to my former supervisor, Professor Claire Squires, for helping me to see what kind of academic I want to be.

From my "second life" as publisher at The Literary Platform, I would like to thank Phyllida Bluemel, Hazel Beevers, Helen Gilchrist and Clare Howdle, brilliant writers and colleagues, one and all. I am also very grateful to Akvile Peckyte, who has been so calm and eagle-eyed. Thanks, too, to Arts Council England, for supporting our work.

I would like to thank all of the novelists, critics, publishers and poets who generously took the time to complete the survey I shared with them in 2019 on the theme of writing culture in a digital age. The views of these award-winning and extraordinarily accomplished writers and journalists—both in the survey and through ongoing conversations—have been invaluable. Notwithstanding those who have requested anonymity, I would like to thank Xan Brooks, Brian Cathcart, Adam Dalton, Emma Darwin, Kit de Waal, Nathan Filer, Liz Flanagan, Jerome Fletcher, Sarah Franklin, Lucille Grant, Alastair Horne, Holly Howitt-Dring, Hanna Jameson, Sam

Leith, Rupert Loydell, Anna Mansell, Alison Jones, Cathy Rentzenbrink, Alice Rooney, Martin Thomas, Luke Thompson, Jack Underwood and Benjamin Wilson.

Thank you to my editors and the production team at Palgrave for their patience and diligence: Brian Halm, Rachel Jacobe, Raghupathy Kalyanaraman, Sarulatha Krishnamurthy, Dr. Jonathan Rose, Dr. Shafquat Towheed and Allie Troyanos.

Last but not least, thank you to my brilliant husband and sons for putting up with my distractedness and supporting me all the while.

Praise for *Writing Cultures and Literary Media*

"In this engaging and timely account, Kiernan reflects on the prospects for contemporary writing cultures in a post-digital, post-COVID world. Drawing on her own unique and varied experiences of the contemporary arts world, as writer, publisher and critic, Kiernan offers refreshing insights not only into the opening up of the cultural industries, but also their shortcomings. This book discusses some of the most innovative writing from recent years, including fiction, nonfiction and poetry, and draws on a wide range of cultural sources including the author's own survey of industry insiders."

—Professor Bronwen Thomas, Head of the Narrative, Culture and Community Research Centre at *Bournemouth University* and author of *Literature and Social Media* (Routledge 2020)

"In this thoughtful and wide-ranging book, Anna Kiernan explores the impact of our digital times on writing both on and off the screen. This timely addition to the scholarship on publishing, storytelling and storytellers is sure to provoke discussion within academia and beyond."

—Sarah Franklin, novelist and Senior Lecturer in Publishing at *Oxford International Centre* for Publishing Studies

"An engaging examination by Anna Kiernan of today's writing cultures. We discover how writers tell their stories in a world of social media, self-publishing and digital consumption. I very much enjoyed the book."

—Angus Phillips, Director of the *Oxford International Centre* for Publishing and author of *Inside Book Publishing* and *Turning the Page*

"This is a pragmatic and richly informed reflection on what literary writing was, is, and might become—both in relation to technology, and in response to emerging societal configurations. An important read for academics, writers and publishers alike."

—Dr. Danielle Barrios-O'Neill, Head of Information Experience Design, *Royal College of Art*

"Kiernan presents a timely perspective of contemporary relationships between reader, author and text. A must read for writers and editors."

—Dr. Amy Lilwall, novelist and Lecturer in Creative Writing, *Lincoln University*

"This fascinating book illuminates a myriad of ways in which digitalization has shaped contemporary literary culture, from criticism and curation to publication and publicity. Kiernan takes a lively, interdisciplinary approach to her subject, referencing a wide range of dynamic writers and thinkers, drawing on her own varied experience in the literary world, and offering plenty of valuable insights."

—Dr. Ellen Wiles, Lecturer in Creative Writing at the *University of Exeter*, novelist and author of *Live Literature: The Experience and Cultural Value of Literary Events from Salons to Festivals* (2021)

CONTENTS

CHAPTER 1

Introduction

In 1762 Jean-Jacques Rousseau declared in *The Social Contract* that "Man is born free, and everywhere he is in chains", a *cri de coeur* that resonated with many Romantic poets and, to some extent, captured the spirit of the age (Rousseau [1762] 2008). At the time of writing (February 2021), the United Kingdom (like many other countries) was under lockdown, which meant that millions of people had to carry out their day to day activities online. Rousseau's words therefore seemed to resonate with new meaning, as our culture of individualism quaked in the wake of state interventions and curtailed freedoms.

What does this have to do with writing culture in a digital age? Pretty much everything. The tension between digital and print has shifted inexorably, due to our dependency on digital. From Zoom meetings at work to livestreamed theatre on YouTube, the element of choice between "live" and online experiences—and therefore the ability to resist digital—has diminished. We are now fully-fledged citizens of a post-digital world—a world in which almost all of our cultural consumption and communication takes place online. Freedoms we previously took for granted, such as going to the library to borrow books, visiting the theatre to watch a show, or wandering around a gallery or museum in our lunch hour, are now characterised by provisos. In this cultural context of constraint, digital writing culture has become less of an option and more of an inevitability.

A. Kiernan, *Writing Cultures and Literary Media*, New Directions in Book History, https://doi.org/10.1007/978-3-030-75081-7_1

But Rousseau's words also speak to the omniscient digital ether that surrounds us. Surveillance capitalism has created an environment in which as we read online we are also being read. In today's usage, the medium is as significant as the message, when we consider the platform for the content being shared. In the fourth quarter of 2020, for instance, Facebook recorded 2.8 billion monthly active users (Tankovska 2020). *The Guardian's* article about Shoshana Zuboff's book, *The Age of Surveillance Capitalism*, explains that, "We're living through the most profound transformation in our information environment since Johannes Gutenberg's invention of printing in circa 1439" (Naughton 2019). Zuboff persuasively suggests that the commodification of communication in the digital world presents a significant threat to democracy, an unprecedented counterpoint to the view that expanding our networks is integral to successful business communication and growth. Our consumer choices, and what we publish on social media (because we are all publishers now), are harvested and reconfigured as data that informs what stories and "stuff" is sold back to us online. This is not a conspiracy theory—rather, it is the reality of an emergent digital public sphere which is, in part, algorithmically determined.

In the context of this unsettling attention economy, we are all, as cyborg anthropologist Sherry Turkle puts it, "alone together"—tethered via our devices but also physically separate (Turkle 2011). David Bolter and Richard Grusin's work on remediation has subsequently taken on new meaning (Bolter and Grusin 2000). Understood most simply as "out with the old, in with the new", the logic of remediation is that an iMac trumps a typewriter because it's faster, better connected and more convenient to use (which goes some way to explaining why Apple superfans queue for hours for the latest iPhone). But the relentless march of consumerism often belies a desire for a life characterised by more intimate encounters and more tangible forms of connectivity. Analogue cultures such as physical books appeal because, in their printed form, they constitute "static content", which temporarily stops us from disappearing down the digital rabbit hole.

What, then, is the reality of writing culture in a digital age? The writing community has adapted and created content for digital consumption in rich and imaginative ways. At times like these, the literary industries can adapt and thrive in ways that aren't available to live, performance-based art forms such as theatre and opera. In terms of the marketplace, lockdown has, to some extent, fuelled the public's appetite for podcasts and audio books. Deloitte predicted that the global market would grow by 25% in 2020 to $3.5 billion (£2.6 billion) and that was *before* the lockdown (Thorp 2020). But, overall, the picture is mixed, as independent bookshops and the usual summer schedule of author events, book festivals and publications have been cancelled or postponed.

While literary culture is currently being experienced in isolation, it should not be viewed in isolation. Rather than focusing on singular texts, this book explores literary media and writing ecologies that are shaped by the "convergence of literary, visual, and material cultures" (Collins 2010, 8; Thomas 2020). The connecting theme in each of the chapters that follow is the relationship between the production and consumption of literary media among audiences for whom digital technology is the primary mode of communication.

Drawing on empirical, sociological and ethnographic insights from contemporary writing and publishing contexts, *Writing Cultures and Literary Media* considers how hierarchies of cultural capital circulate on, and in relation to, the internet. In a pre-digital public sphere the conversation was less fluid: "ordinary people—the public—[were] cast in the role of audience members who [were] merely able to watch the events unfolding on this 'virtual stage of mediated communication'" (Bruns and Highfield 2015). Now, they can respond in real time and speak directly to the powers that be (from editors to world leaders) via Twitter and Instagram, thus opening up the potential for storytelling across platforms and boundaries.

Storytelling is the lifeblood of the creative industries and is of course second nature to writers, publishers, poets and playwrights. The range of platforms and formats through which we can consume and publish content and engage with others has broadened our understanding of what it means to be a reader and a writer. But these cultural shifts are not without consequences: authors who are busy with the shadow-work of promoting themselves online find it ever more challenging to finish writing their books. Digital has created a huge range of new opportunities for creating and writing but it seems as though there's no time to do it in. These are just some of the themes alluded to by the authors, journalists and critics who responded to an online survey I conducted in 2019. Totalling more than 10,000 words of impassioned, astute and sometimes acerbic qualitative commentary and quantitative insights, the general consensus among respondents seemed to be that being a writer is at once exhilarating (in terms of engagement and diversity) and overwhelming (in terms of the volume of content and the demise of gatekeepers) (see appendix). The respondents' insights, as well as ongoing conversations with authors and editors, frame and inform each of the chapters in this book.

This enquiry into the habits and views of writers, particularly with reference to the impact of social media on literary production and reception, is informed by an abiding interest in literary ethnography. In her book *Live Literature* (2021), Ellen Wiles defines "experiential literary ethnography" as a practice intended to both evoke and examine creative literary experiences. Her first-person account of live literature events foregrounds the "merits of experiential literary ethnography" inasmuch as that her encounters seem central to her practice (Wiles 2021, 16). This approach has informed my own reflections on weaving in and out of publishing and the literary industries over the last twenty years within a self-reflexive ethnographic practice (Wiles 2021, 16).

As an assistant editor at André Deutsch publishing in the 1990s, I worked on typed manuscripts scattered with seemingly cryptic proofreading marks across folios that had been delivered from the typesetter by courier. Now, of course, we edit online and author files are shared instantly, the paper trail having dried up. The piles of collated proofs heaped haphazardly in the corners of editors' offices in Bloomsbury have long-since been recycled, archived or mythologised in memoirs. As a publisher twenty years on, my workload has expanded from writing and editing to creating and sharing content, and it is these sorts of shifts which inform the practice-based approach to research in this book. To borrow the words of literary sociologist Robert Darnton, my approach embraces "a riot of interdisciplinarity" because, like many professional writers, editors and creatives, I have worked across many disciplines. But as Wiles suggests, in the academy (where colleagues are often defined by their specialism) this process is perhaps understandably sometimes greeted with a degree of distrust: "Creative approaches to academic writing are characterised by scholars who distrust them as soft or insufficiently rigorous, implying simplicity or ease" (Wiles 2021, 270).

In "The Impossible Constellation: Practice as Research as a Viable Alternative" Sarah Barrow notes that such "creative approaches" are the bedrock of practice-based research. With reference to the field of publishing studies, Barrow notes that this "impossible constellation" has yet to be fully assimilated into the academy, suggesting that unless the stars are aligned—or the dots connected—along the lines of preexisting, peer-reviewed research (so, the field), they may be refuted or rejected by academics within that field. Barrow addresses this problem, explaining that practice as research "is a kind of 'practical knowing-in-doing', where insight, methodological rigour and originality are key, and might be shared with and learnt from other practice-based disciplines such as education and ethnography" (Barrow 2016, 25; Smith and Dean 2009). She concludes that practice constitutes research because it becomes in and of itself "a key method of inquiry" (Barrow 2016, 25).

Practice-based methods of identifying patterns of cultural participation remain a central concern in my professional experience (as a writer, editor and publisher) in literary culture. This book draws together contemporary case studies and practitioner insights that epitomise a particular moment in the development of the post-digital literary landscape. It discusses these examples both in relation to their conditions of production and in relation to the ways in which the narrative encounter—so how the text is engaged with, and via which media or platform—affects how the text might be received (by critics and general readers).

Chapter 2, "Writing Culture and Cultural Value", introduces literary culture in terms of how value is ascribed within the field of cultural production. It is concerned with the construction of different forms of cultural capital, specifically in relation to publishing case studies that can be seen to epitomise the balancing act of sustaining economic and social capital. The discussion that follows therefore explores the dynamic relationship between the conditions of literary production and the players within that changing literary landscape. The anatomy of the field is determined in part by the logic of the constituent elements of cultural capital but, in terms of the field of restricted production and the field of large-scale production, the dynamic has shifted with the advent of digital communication.

Chapter 3, "Critics and Curators in a Socially Networked Age", considers the ways in which literary and cultural criticism differ from crowdsourced and online reviews, and is concerned with the changing role of gatekeepers in the context of online critics and curators. It discusses the heritage of contemporary understandings of literary criticism, from the New Criticism to Reader-Response criticism, and considers the impact of social media on cultures of criticism. In this chapter, the anatomy of reviews is reviewed and the future of criticism is, as it were, critiqued.

Chapter 4, "Diversity, Representation and Innovation in Online Literary Promotion", considers the ways in which writers of colour are published in the UK and the promotional opportunities that might be further explored to grow audiences online in order to diversify commissioning practices. Drawing on research conducted by Goldsmiths University, in partnership with *The Bookseller* magazine and writer development agency Spread the Word, this chapter revisits post colonial theory in relation to contemporary London novels and discusses forward-facing case studies that move beyond a monocultural industry narrative.

Chapter 5, "Instagram, Poetry and the Politics of Emotion", continues with this focus on institutional contexts in its discussion of literary gatekeepers. Writers with a propensity for building a personal brand and sharing their stories on social media have, to some extent, changed the way that poetry is consumed and engaged with. In Chap. 5, I discuss the implications of this debate in terms of gendered cultural production and consider the relevance of the role of cultural influencers for the future of publishing. With reference to Rebecca Watts' article in *PN Review* (2018), which critiqued poets such as Hollie McNish, this chapter considers how poetry as an art form is responding to the challenges posed by shifts in publishing norms.

Chapter 6, "From Fidelity Publishing to Playable Stories", discusses genre in relation to digital experiments, immersive texts and gamified literary media, with reference to examples ranging from Stephen King's digital-first novella *UR* to Charlie Brooker's Netflix drama *Bandersnatch*. It begins by identifying the "pleasure of the familiar" as an ongoing challenge for publishing, in terms of form, content and audiences, then focuses on case studies that have captured the attention of audiences by playing with preconceived ideas of experience and engagement at the intersection of literature and technology. The preoccupying theme in this chapter is the rise of convergence culture as a catalyst for moving beyond the assumed binary division between the "threat" of digital and print.

Chapter 7 examines contemporary literary case studies, in which authors grapple with emotional exposure and the promotional pressures of revealing (or concealing) their "authentic" selves. With a focus on the narrative tension that emerges from the interplay between fiction and non-fiction, this chapter considers how texts such as Karl Ove Knausgård's six autobiographical novels and Megan Boyle's *Liveblog*, which has been described as Alt Lit, can be seen to exhibit interior identities seemingly untrammelled by social boundaries. It is therefore interested in the relationship between autofiction and online communication as imperfect indicators of "authenticity" in an era characterised by the demise of cultural gatekeepers online.

Chapter 8, "Materiality and Post-Digital Storytelling", draws on insights from cross-disciplinary case studies, from small press editions and artefacts to passion-project publishing. This is, in a sense, the antidote chapter—a place in which to consider counterpoints to seemingly inevitable digital outcomes by exploring outlier examples of writing culture that stir passion among collectors and producers alike, in order to reevaluate what it means to innovate in a (post) digital age.

I would like to conclude this introduction with some provisos. I drew on many periodical-based (as well as peer-reviewed) sources in writing this book because, in this fast-changing digital world, these case studies sometimes provided the most up-to-date viewpoints and market developments. Given the range of subject matter, more questions are raised than answered: digital culture is amorphous and in flux, so the conversation remains open ended. *Writing Cultures and Literary Media* explores a world in which words, images, texts, platforms and stories variously coalesce and collide. The experiences and insights of my contemporaries, who have so generously shared some of the stories *behind* the stories that they write and publish, resonate with these preoccupations and interrogate the diminishing space for the private writing self in these very public publishing times.

REFERENCES

Barrow, Sarah. 2016. The Impossible Constellation: Practice as Research as a Viable Alternative. In *The Academic Book of the Future*, ed. Rebecca E. Lyons and Samantha Rayner. Basingstoke: Palgrave.

Bolter, J.D., and R. Grusin. 2000. *Remediation: Understanding New Media*. Cambridge, MA: MIT.

Bruns, Alex, and Alex Highfield. 2015. Is Habermas on Twitter? Social Media and the Public Sphere. In *The Routledge Companion to Social Media and Politics*, ed. Enli Gunn, Axel Bruns, Christian Christensen, Anders Olof Larsson, and Eli Skogerbo. Taylor and Francis. https://eprints.qut.edu.au/91810/42/__ qut.edu.au_Documents_StaffHome_staffgroupB%24_bozzetto_ Documents_2016000110_chapter.pdf. Accessed 20 Feb 2021.

Collins, J. 2010. *Bring on the Books for Everybody: How Literary Culture Became Popular Culture*. Durham: Duke University Press.

Jones, Philip. 2015. A Year of Living Digital. *Bookseller*, December 22. Available at https://www.thebookseller.com/futurebook/year-living-digital-318805. Accessed 10 June 2018.

Naughton, John. 2019. The Goal Is to Automate Us: Welcome to the Age of Surveillance Capitalism. *The Guardian*, January 20. https://www.theguardian.com/technology/2019/jan/20/shoshana-zuboff-age-of-surveillance-capitalism-google-facebook Accessed 30 June 2019.

Rousseau, Jean-Jacques. 2008. *The Social Contract*. Oxford: Oxford University Press.

Smith, Hazel, and Roger T. Dean. 2009. *Practice-Led Research, Research-Led Practice in the Creative Arts*. Edinburgh: Edinburgh University Press.

Tankovska, H. 2020. Number of Monthly Active Facebook Users Worldwide as of 4th Quarter 2020. *Statista*, February 2. https://www.statista.com/statistics/264810/number-of-monthly-active-facebook-users-worldwide/ Accessed 20 Feb 2021.

Thomas, B. 2020. Personal Correspondence. 16 July 2020.

Thorp, Clare. 2020. Audiobooks: The Rise and Rise of the Books You Don't Read. *BBC*, January 6. Available at https://www.bbc.com/culture/article/20200104-audiobooks-the-rise-and-rise-of-the-books-you-dont-read?referer=https%3A%2F%2Fwww.google.com%2F. Accessed 10 June 2020.

Turkle, Sherry. 2011. *Alone Together: Why We Expect More from Technology and Less from Each Other*. New York: Basic Books.

Watts, Rebecca. 2018. The Cult of the Noble Amateur. *PN Review 239* 44 (3). https://www.pnreview.co.uk/cgi-bin/scribe?item_id=10090. Accessed 25 July 2019.

Wiles, Ellen. 2021. *Live Literature: The Experience and Cultural Value of Literary Performance Events from Salons to Festivals*. Basingstoke: Palgrave.

Zuboff, Shoshana. 2019. *The Age of Surveillance Capitalism: The Fight for a Human Future at the New Frontier of Power*. London: Profile.

CHAPTER 2

Writing Culture and Cultural Value

I'm sceptical that the 'democratisation of culture' is really taking place, but in principle would be in favour of that. (David Devanny, 2019)

It is through the interplay of economic and symbolic capital that book publishing and the literary industries have historically found traction, since to have money but no network is almost as unavailing as having a notable reputation but no money. As John B. Thompson explains in *Merchants of Culture: The Publishing Business in the Twenty-First Century*: "For most trade publishers, the 'value' of a particular book or book project is understood in one of two ways: its sales [economic capital]…its quality [symbolic capital]" (Thompson 2010, 10). This understanding correlates with Pierre Bourdieu's work on the field of cultural production, which situates creative outputs in the context of the social conditions of their production and consumption:

> the field of production per se owes its own structure to the opposition between the field of restricted production as a system producing cultural goods (and the instruments for appropriating these goods) objectively designed for a public of producers of cultural goods, and the field of large scale cultural production, specially organized with a view to the production of cultural goods destined for non-producers of cultural goods, "the public at large." (Bourdieu 1993, 115)

© The Author(s), under exclusive license to Springer Nature Switzerland AG 2021
A. Kiernan, *Writing Cultures and Literary Media*, New Directions in Book History, https://doi.org/10.1007/978-3-030-75081-7_2

In terms of book publishing, the field of restricted production is particularly relevant to specialist small press ventures that create limited edition books with high production values. Such publishers range from esteemed publishers such as The Hogarth Press, which Leonard and Virginia Woolf founded in 1917, to Visual Editions, a contemporary creative agency whose predominantly digital portfolio includes limited edition publishing experiments. In "The New Reading Public: Modernism, Popular Literature and the Paperbacks", Vike Plock discusses the field of restricted production in relation to the first edition of James Joyce's novel *Ulysses* (1922), which had a limited print run of 1000. Such collectible texts signify the "rise to the status of cultural objects endowed with an economic value" in a similar way to artworks, with a first edition of *Ulysses*, for instance, fetching £275,000 at auction (Plock 2019; Bourdieu 1993, 97). More recently, the challenge of publishing *Tree of Codes*, an intricate die-cut sculptural object (or book) by Jonathan Safran Foer, formed the basis of the marketing campaign for Visual Editions (Faber 2010) (see Chap. 8 for more on this text). Therefore, while its success was bound up in its exclusivity within the restricted field (it currently retails at around £200), *Tree of Codes* reached its audience through digital communication, specifically via a short promotional film made about the printing process which has garnered more than 83,000 views on YouTube.

Cultural Capital

As Sarah Brouillette and Christopher Doody put it so well in their chapter "The Literary as a Cultural Industry": "literary scholars have embraced Bourdieu's work because of the tribute it pays to literature as the lynchpin of the 'autonomous field,' where value and wealth are accrued almost despite themselves" (Brouillette and Doody 2015, 1). This chapter considers their playful phrase "almost despite themselves", which can be read as suggesting that publishing is a cultural industry that has survived even though publishing business models are not always as robust as those of other cultural industries (such as film and advertising). Trade publishing and the literary industries have historically been fuelled by passion, personalities, and, at times, private incomes. The discussion that follows therefore explores the relationship between the conditions of literary production and the cultural intermediaries (or publishing players) who inhabit the changing literary landscape.

In *Merchants of Culture: The Publishing Business in the Twenty-First Century* (2010), sociologist John B. Thompson's understanding of capital derives from Bourdieu's notion of the field—that "structured space of social positions"—which defines how the outcomes of cultural endeavours are perceived and communicated to prospective audiences (Thompson 2010, 4–5). As Thompson explains: "The logic of the field is like the grammar of a language: individuals know how to speak correctly, and in this sense they have a practical knowledge of the rules of grammar" (Thompson 2010).

Thompson draws on Pierre Bourdieu's *Distinction: A Social Critique of the Judgement of Taste* in which Bourdieu identifies three forms of capital (social, economic and cultural) that influence interactions within a particular field and signify hierarchical power relations. Thompson goes on to build on this triad, with reference to human, intellectual and symbolic capital (Bourdieu 1984, 66: Thompson 2010, 5). Symbolic capital is the least tangible, consisting as it does of attributes such as "prestige, recognition and respect accorded to certain individuals and institutions" (see Bourdieu, *Language and Symbolic Power*, ed. John B Thompson, 1991).

Bourdieu asserts that sociologists should conduct their work with an awareness of the implications of their own social position, in terms of attributing value to the work in question. In *The Inheritors: French Students and Their Relations to Culture*, for example, Bourdieu observes that academics tend to assess students' work against an expectation of restrictive linguistic expression and register (or tone of voice), preferring submissions that appear "polished" and marking down those guilty of "vulgarity" (Bourdieu and Passeron 1979, 20–4). In today's literary marketplace, the tension between "polished" and "vulgar", highbrow and popular culture persists, with digital-first writing and blended publishing models often being aligned with the field of "large-scale cultural production" as opposed to the field of restricted production.

BLENDED PUBLISHING MODELS

The field of "large-scale cultural production" is predicated on a commercial imperative for low-risk, low-cost, large-scale outputs intended for established audiences. In book form, this commonly takes the form of paperback genre fiction, such as romances and detective fiction;

publications that were "intended to ensure a rapid return of profit through rapid or mass circulation of products with built in obsolescence" (Bourdieu 1993, 97). Audio book purchases via Amazon's Audible, as well as ebooks, are similarly designed with built-in obsolescence in mind and are more likely to be consumed and disposed of like glossy magazines, rather than collected and displayed as signifiers of cultural capital on bookshelves.

While most publishers would of course prefer each title they publish to make a profit, having a foot in both camps, as it were, can be challenging. With reference to the Hogarth Press, Woolf believed that "content should precede material aesthetics" (McTaggart 2010, 63) but, despite this, acknowledged the importance of a creating a brand identity, a key aspect of commercial publishing which shapes the relation to the market (Gordon 2010, 193). Thus, the creation of a new logo in 1928 signalled a "move towards a cooperative relationship with mass publishing" (Plock 2019, 141). Woolf's pragmatism is relevant to the hybrid approach of some of the more tenacious contemporary publishers, in its acceptance of the need to perpetually reimagine the potential for publications to reach emergent audiences (if money is to be made).

Risk and Restricted Production

Some contemporary small publishers of bespoke illustrated books, such as Steve Braund at Atlantic Press Books and Luke Thompson at Guillemot Press, have expressed to me their commitment to publishing limited edition books regardless of profit margins. The precarity implied by such high-risk endeavours has become well documented over recent years through accounts of the plight of small publishers struggling with the demands of corporate distribution partners. Galley Beggar Press founders Sam Jordison and Eloise Millar, for instance, raised more than £42,000 in under twenty-four hours in 2019, thus saving them from insolvency after their distributor, The Book People, went into administration (Wood 2019). Again, while the emphasis of Jordison's public plea was on the potential loss in their ability to produce high-quality print publications (their lists include titles such as Lucy Ellmann's *Ducks, Newburyport*, which was shortlisted for the Booker Prize 2019), the promotional campaign that resulted in the crowdfunding target being met took place on Twitter, a platform upon which Jordison's journalistic storytelling skills secured the attention of an audience befitting Bourdieu's description of "a public of producers of cultural goods" (Bourdieu 1993, 115), in other words, cultural producers (such as writers) and intermediaries (such as journalists and critics). This example of a small press publisher continuing against all odds epitomises Brouillette and Doody's suggestion that some publishers are able to continue to exist "almost despite themselves" (Brouillette and Doody 2015, 1). Social media has therefore become an invaluable platform for publishers seeking to publicise their products (or plight, in the case of Galley Beggar Press) for free, thus allowing them to continue to operate within the restricted field of cultural production.

INTUITION AND BRAND BUILDING

While the "field of restricted production" can, broadly speaking, appear to be less driven by business objectives than trade publishing, even the Hogarth Press eventually recognised the need to "transition from a coterie Bloomsbury handpress to a proper publishing business" (Southworth 2010, 19). Thompson's interviews with more mainstream publishers reveal a comparable viewpoint in terms of editorial decision making, in which, at times, the economic rationale follows the aesthetic rationale (rather than dictating it):

> To justify buying a book we have to fill out a profit and loss statement…so I'm supposed to know how many copies we're going to print, how many pictures we're going to have, what paper's going to cost, what the price is going to be, and most important, how good it is. Well, it's clearly a wank— there's no way that any possible person can do it. And so you say to your assistant, 'we're spending $50,000. Work up figures that make sense and stick them in.' Everybody knows they're lies. (Thompson 2010, 131)

This candid insight into the intuitive trade publishing commissioning process is also evident in "Rethinking 'Diversity' in Publishing", a report in which Anamik Saha and Sandra van Lente cite similar findings from their interviews with publishers:

> Indeed, a quote by one senior, white publisher alludes to how data, while regarded as objective and neutral, is used creatively to back up editors' own agendas: 'they tend to take the bits of it that they like and discount the rest'. In this way, one gets a sense of how data used during the comping process can be used to confirm a particular bias.' (Saha and van Lente 2020: 19)

Creative data interpretation and comping, a publishing practice which involves identifying market trends and following them, are commonplace among trade publishing commissioning editors, as Saha and van Lente's research suggests. The problem is that while comping is integral to building genre fiction lists, which are necessarily repetitive in terms of themes and characters, comping other forms of literature and writing can be seen to promote the continuation of exclusionary cultural practices (which is discussed further in Chap. 4).

In the balancing act between sustaining economic and social capital, economic risk can sometimes be tolerated if the symbolic gain (understood most simply as brand building) is deemed to be sufficiently rewarding.[1] Thompson's understanding of capital derives from Bourdieu's notion of the field—that "structured space of social positions"—which defines how the outcomes of cultural endeavours are perceived and communicated to prospective audiences (Thompson 2010, 4). This fascination with the idea of embodied symbolic capital, in which well-connected (networked) cultural intermediaries have the ability to influence, is a recurring focus of *Merchants of Culture* and in some ways seems out of step with the contemporary sense of disillusionment with the privileged traditional gatekeepers within the literary industries, who are likely to be in possession of elusive symbolic capital (Thompson 2010, 12). Symbolic capital retains an aura of mystery born of economic capital, inasmuch as that the confidence to acquire social capital is oftentimes a feature of privilege, which is sometimes expressed through cultural stereotypes of old fashioned publishers as being gifted, eccentric and privileged. Representations of this kind find form in memoirs such as "mad genius" Tom Maschler's *Publisher* and Diana Athill's deliciously indiscreet memoir, *Stet* (2011) (Wroe 2005).[2]

---

[1] For example, this is evident in the publication of *A Room of One's Own* by Virginia Woolf in 1929. Hogarth Press initially published the book at a price of five shillings, then went on to release a limited, special edition priced at two pounds and two shillings. As Vike Plock suggests, this shows that with this publication, the Hogarth Press was "hoping to [both] appeal to collectors and to consumers with more limited means" (Plock 2019, 142).

[2] Former journalist and publishing studies academic Susan Greenberg's insightful edited collection of interviews in *Editors Talk about Editing: Insights for Readers, Writers and Publishers* (2015) romanticises the industry a little less, but this may be partly because some of the publishers referenced are from an academic publishing background rather than a trade publishing one.

LITERARY SOCIOLOGY

Human-centred stories are both the beating heart of literary sociology and the publishing industry itself, and the romanticisation of the industry forms a through line in biographical references to the book trade. Late in the last century, in a provocative article titled "Publishing History: A Hole at the Centre of Literary Sociology", John Sutherland labelled research into publishing history as "incompetent" (Sutherland 1988, 575), which appears to be in part a response to subjective depictions of the field, through, for instance, the sorts of biographical accounts referenced above. At the time (the 1980s), publishing studies was emerging as a discrete discipline that is now well established within the academy, though it is still subject to a degree of categorical uncertainty among academics who view the segue into ethnographic and journalistic methodologies as being out of kilter with the more tightly structured domain of publishing history. In his lively discussion of Darnton's sociological account of the world of books in Paris in the eighteenth century, Sutherland cites Darnton's description of publishing history as a "riot of interdisciplinarity", suggesting that it should be "disciplined" (ibid).

The acerbic tone of Sutherland's assertion is laced with affection, though, since Sutherland (himself a literary biographer) appears to enjoy Darnton's colourful account a great deal. Sutherland therefore draws attention to the view that, broadly speaking, the history of book publishing can be a rather stolid affair, which may be partly why Robert Darnton's account of "The Literary Underground of the Old Regime" continues to attract attention. As a cultural historian, Darnton's work brings to life the "characters" who moved through the Parisian publishing landscape in technicolour: "Joseph Duplain ('one of the scrappiest book dealers in one of the toughest towns of the book trade'); Charles-Joseph Panckoucke ('the aggressive publisher from Lille'), are characters who came to dominate the Parisian trade" (Sutherland 1988, 579). This account of the book trade is almost as sensory and evocative as Patrick Suskind's novel *Perfume*, in terms of the amorous attachment that Darnton's characters feel for their stock-in-trade. Underpinned by an interest in the ideological origins of the French Revolution, Darnton's portraits of publishing "players" can be read as testimony to Clifford and Marcus' assertion in *Writing Culture: The Poetics and Politics of Ethnography* that "the poetic and the political are inseparable" (Clifford and Marcus 2010, 30). These ethnographic sketches also foreground the relationships between particular individuals, which have been so central to the formation of this idiosyncratic industry (book publishing) and which animates writing culture in ways that a more detailed transactional analysis of print runs and sales figures might overlook. In effect, Darnton's sketches reveal that the literary industries are complicated due to the proximate relationship between the producer, the text and the consumer. Writing culture is therefore the outcome of the dialogue between consumer and producer, in relation to the text.

In *Keywords: A Vocabulary of Culture and Society*, Raymond Williams said that "Culture is one of the two or three most complicated words in the English language" both because of its historical development as a Western ideological construct and because of its entrenched interdisciplinarity, complete with "incompatible systems of thought" (Williams 1988). Entrenched interdisciplinary is resistant to simplistic binary oppositions such as public/private, story/narrative and digital/print. Viewed through an interdisciplinary lens, literary media, from Tweets and text messages to "letters…and narratives inhering in objects" are all texts that can be critically analysed and ethnographically unpicked (Andrews, Squire and Tamboukou 2008, 5). The point of difference in terms of interpreting such stories is the question of whether they should be read as revealing only "internal individual states, or external social circumstances" (Ibid) or both. The penned markers of selfhood are as much in evidence in writing for the public, through journalism, publishing and social media, as through stories of everyday life expressed through journals, notes and lists. The act of writing, publishing and story-sharing cannot be neutral since stories are born into a system of cultural value that decodes narrative in relation to its mode of production.

In their article "The Digital Publishing Communications Circuit", Claire Squires and Padmini Ray Murray reconsider Darnton's model of communication within its structural (rather than sociological) context, stating that: "Robert Darnton envisioned the journey of textual transmission from author to reader as the communications circuit which depicted the role of different agents in the value chain such as printers, publishers and booksellers" (Squires and Ray 2013). They go on to propose a reconfigured version of the communication circuit for the digital age—one which designates a relationship (that has the potential to leapfrog cultural intermediaries such as agents and critics) not only between the author and their audience but also, it seems, between the publisher and their readers.

CONCLUSION

The idea that our social position is likely to prejudice our literary preferences is now widely accepted (often in the context of the assumed divide between highbrow and popular culture) but the nuances and implications of such social relations remain a work in progress, in terms of both form and content. Exploring the frameworks for attributing cultural value to literary culture, with reference to representation and identity, offers a way of better understanding writing culture in a digital age.

The anatomy of the field is determined in part by the logic of the constituent elements of cultural capital but, in terms of the field of restricted production and the field of large-scale production, the dynamic has shifted with the advent of digital communication. A literary text can be understood as constituting a link in the value chain but so too can a film of the literary text's production process (in the case of *Tree of Codes*) or a social media promotional campaign (in the case of Galley Beggar Press). In this way, the digital campaign reinforces the value of the printed text and vice versa. The reconfigured communication circuit therefore does more than simply reevaluate the relationship between the producer and the consumer; it interrupts the sequential nature of the value chain and the associated bastions of cultural capital and privilege. The next chapter explores this idea further, with reference to the changing role of cultural gatekeepers such as critics and curators in a digital age.

REFERENCES

Andrews, Molly, Corinne Squire, and Maria Tamboukou, eds. 2008. *Doing Narrative Research*. London: Sage.

Bourdieu, Pierre. 1984. *Distinction: A Social Critique of the Judgment of Taste*. Trans. Richard Nice. Cambridge, MA: Harvard University Press.

———. 1993. *The Field of Cultural Production*. Cambridge: Polity Press.

Bourdieu, Pierre, and Jean-Claude Passeron. 1979 [1964]. *The Inheritors: French Students and Their Relations to Culture*. Chicago: University of Chicago Press.

Brouillette, Sarah, and Christopher Doody. 2015. The Literary as a Cultural Industry. In *The Routledge Companion to the Culture Industries*, ed. Kate Oakley and Justin O'Connor, 99–109. Abingdon-on-Thames: Routledge.

Clifford, James, and George Marcus. 2010. *Writing Culture: The Poetics and Politics of Ethnography*. 25th Anniversary Edition. Berkeley: University of California Press.

Devanny, David. 2019. This quote is from an online survey I ran between January and March 2019 (See Appendix).

Faber, Michael. 2010. Tree of Codes by Jonathan Safran Foer – Review. *The Guardian*, December 18. https://www.theguardian.com/books/2010/dec/18/tree-codes-safran-foer-review. Accessed 2 Mar 2021.

Gordon, Elizabeth Willson. 2010. On or About December 1928 the Hogarth Press Changed: E. McKnight Kauffer, Art, Markets and the Hogarth Press 1928–39. In *Leonard and Virginia Woolf, the Hogarth Press and the Networks of Modernism*, ed. Helen Southworth. Edinburgh: Edinburgh University Press.

McTaggart, Ursula. 2010. 'Opening the Door': The Hogarth Press as Virginia Woolf's Outsiders' Society. *Tulsa Studies in Women's Literature* 29 (1): 63–81.

Plock, Vike. 2019. The New Reading Public: Modernism, Popular Literature and the Paperbacks. In *A History of 1930s British Literature*, ed. Benjamin Kohlmann and Matthew Taunton. Cambridge: Cambridge University Press.

Saha, Anamik, and Sandra van Lente. 2020. *Rethinking 'Diversity' in Publishing*. London: Goldsmiths Press.

Southworth, Helen, ed. 2010. *Leonard and Virginia Woolf, the Hogarth Press and the Networks of Modernism*. Edinburgh: Edinburgh University Press.

Squires, C., and Murray P. Ray. 2013. The Digital Publishing Communications Circuit. *Book 2.0* 3 (1): 3–24. https://doi.org/10.1386/btwo.3.1.3_1.

Sutherland, John. 1988. Publishing History: A Hole at the Centre of Literary Sociology. *The Sociology of Literature* 14 (3, Spring): 574–589.

Thompson, John B. 2010. *Merchants of Culture: The Publishing Business in the Twenty-First Century*. Cambridge: Polity.

Williams, Raymond. 1988. *Keywords: A Vocabulary of Culture and Society*. Oxford: Oxford University Press.

Wood, Heloise. 2019. Galley Beggar Press 'Saved' After Crowd Funder Raises £42k. *The Bookseller*, December 19. https://www.thebookseller.com/news/galley-beggar-press-book-people-administration-crowdfunder. Accessed 2 Mar 2021.

Wroe, Nicholas. 2005. Talent Spotter. *The Guardian*, March 12. https://www.theguardian.com/books/2005/mar/12/featuresreviews.guardianreview14. Accessed 2 Mar 2021.

CHAPTER 3

Critics and Curators in a Socially Networked Age

A working democracy needs both academic critical work and a lively, unfettered popular culture. The problem I see in our contemporary culture (and since the late eighteenth century), is the lack of respect and communication between the two. This gap is about power in both directions and is related to the current 'democratic deficit' we are experiencing in the west, I think. (Meredith Miller 2019)[1]

Critics and curators have historically been gatekeepers within the creative and cultural industries. Both professions carry with them the weight of authority, of having earned their place as arbiters of taste and filters of knowledge. They share the umbrella role of being cultural intermediaries—that is to say, taste makers who contribute to the discourses and definitions of what counts as worthy of a wider audience, whether that be in a library or museum, gallery or the review pages of a newspaper.

Drawing these distinct categories of cultural intermediary together (each of which possesses different skills and attributes) is significant in its tendency to concurrently expand and reduce the discrete values of both. Disentangling the two becomes problematic as a result of the democratisation of writing culture, in which anyone with access to the Internet can

---

[1] This quote is from the survey I conducted between January and March 2019 (see Appendix).

© The Author(s), under exclusive license to Springer Nature Switzerland AG 2021
A. Kiernan, *Writing Cultures and Literary Media*, New Directions in Book History, https://doi.org/10.1007/978-3-030-75081-7_3

share their views online, a space in which the critic and the curator are conflated. This etymological shift inevitably affects the cultural value of both ventures.

This chapter discusses contemporary understandings of cultural curation and criticism. Drawing on case studies that illuminate the tension between traditional gatekeepers and digital influencers, it considers how the framework of reference for attributing value has changed in an era of convergence culture and digital communications.

CULTURAL CURATORS

In *Textual Curation: Authorship, Agency, and Technology in Wikipedia and Chamber's Cyclopaedia,* Krista Kennedy explores and revises "commonly held cultural notions of what constitutes both authorship and writing" as a means of establishing "new" textual activities such as wikis with a long-standing authorial practice that she calls "textual curation" (Kennedy 2016, 22). Kennedy contends that the relatively new concept of distributed authorship in the humanities actually has a long tradition within the co-creation of major publishing projects such as dictionaries. Sites such as Wikipedia form the sort of frequently cited contemporary manifestations of digital distributed authorship but are characterised by the validation of amateurism which is indicative of the cultural shift towards the hive mind offering up opinions online. This shift is closely aligned to the exponential growth of online reviews which so many consumers consult before buying (or buying into) an idea, experience or object. Clusters of reviews and comment trails constitute what can be termed distributed criticism, with the accumulation of consensus in these spaces becoming largely self-perpetuating. In this way, cultural curation and reviewing have become entwined, as the qualifying definitions of both terms are eroded. This has had significant implications for how crowd-sourced websites are run and how critical content is produced and consumed.

The emergent behaviours arising from the evolution of the term curation has resulted in a sense of unease within the de-professionalised ranks of the experts, as Kennedy notes in her definition of the field: "Curation is a specialized craft and field of study in multiple curation-focused disciplines that award advanced degrees, train specialists, launch distinguished careers, and create robust scholarship" (Kennedy 2016, 5). Extolling the virtues of the gatekeepers could be regarded as an insufficient defence against the content avalanche online. Remediated and refined, the definition itself has adapted to reflect the characteristics of a changing digital humanities landscape, which is evident in UCLA's influential Digital Humanities Manifesto 2.0:

> Curation means making arguments through objects as well as words, images, and sounds. It implies a spatialization of the sort of critical and narrative tasks that, while not unfamiliar to historians, are fundamentally different when carried out in space—physical, virtual, or both—rather than in language alone. (UCLA n.d.)

Curation within the digital humanities is now characterised by dynamic, interactive, immersive encounters rather than static descriptive narrative accounts. In the past, experts curated exhibitions in museums and galleries; in the present, platforms such as Instagram, Tripadvisor and Facebook encourage "prosumers" to co-curate representations of experiences (which may or may not include gallery visits) on their personal pages.[2]

Selection and interpretation (still) lies at the heart of curation, though knotty questions regarding ownership, agency, authority and authenticity remain to be disentangled. In the past, curating historically enacted the discourses of power, particularly during the nineteenth century, an era in which the classification of objects was matched only by the obsession with data that characterises algorithmic behaviours and decision making on the web today (Houser 2020; Ritvo 1998). It also signified "symbolic capital", which, as John B. Thompson explains in *Merchants of Culture*, "is best understood as the accumulated prestige, recognition and respect accorded to certain individuals and institutions". He goes on to explain that symbolic capital is an "intangible asset" afforded to "cultural mediators" (Thompson 2010, 8). Cultural gatekeepers acquire symbolic capital through the roles that they perform. Symbolic capital can be garnered through social media campaigns that promote engagement with particular products or ideas, through content curation, which short cuts the process of accruing capital within Thompson's value chain, in which social and economic advantages are a prerequisite for the accumulation of such intangible assets.

---

[2] In 2011, Facebook went so far as to automatically generate individual galleries of "memories" from its users' digital lives, by creating a virtual Museum of Me, an action that would likely be greeted with a greater level of scepticism today.

Within the creative and cultural industries, the term curator has become malleable through "language in use". Platforms such as Pinterest, Instagram and Facebook offer spaces upon which to forge an aesthetically determined identity made up of colour-coded photos and sketches which showcase "moments", memories or influences as a way of communicating narratives of commodified emotion and style. Such platforms become the galleries of their individual users and display their cultural capital through symbolic association. Books such as *My Ideal Bookshelf* (La force 2012) emulate the encoded repetition that characterises the behaviour of hashtagging social media users. With #bookshelfies from postmodern novelists including Jennifer Egan and Miranda July, the illustrated book signifies a sense of style amplified by social settings (La Force 2012). As content strategist Eileen Mullan explains:

> Content curation is all around us. It can take the form of an RSS feed, links posted on blogs, social media feeds, or an online news mashup like the ECDaily...Many of us have been participating in content curation for years without even knowing it. Anyone with a Facebook feed or Twitter stream has seen content curation first hand. (Mullan 2011)

Content curation has become a loaded term, both in terms of its historical agenda and its contemporary significance and as a form of self-expression, personal branding and style (Hebdige 1979; Wilcox 2020). The role of the traditional gatekeeper-curator within this changing digital landscape has become less secure, not simply as a result of online influencers but also because the democratisation of the process of curating content has thrown up the question of diversifying audiences and engagement. The art of curation, like criticism, has its roots in technical expertise and a deep understanding of niche disciplines. Curation and content curation are not in competition, as it were—but the advent of the latter risks eclipsing the nuanced insights of the former, in much the same way that online reader reviews often trump professional critics' views in terms of engagement.

READER-RESPONSE CRITICISM

Such tensions—between professional judgement and dilettante opinion— have a long tradition within literary criticism. The advent of Reader-Response Criticism in the wake of the New Criticism is a case in point. According to Lois Tyson, the New Critics "believed that the timeless meaning of the text—what the text is—is contained in the text alone. Its meaning is not a product of the author's intention and does not change with the reader's response" (Tyson 2006, 176). Tyson goes on to compare this to Reader-Response theory, which proposes that "what a text is cannot be separated from what it does" (Tyson 2006, 176). As such, one of the significant points of difference between the New Criticism and Reader-Response Criticism is that the former can be viewed as more detached and passive, while the latter is more involved and immediate, in terms of the perceived relationship between the text and its reader(s). The former seems to favour pre-determination, while the latter is seemingly more open ended.

In *Reading the Romance* (1984) Janice Radway showed that the Reader-Response approach can also serve as an ethnographic tool capable of heat-mapping the reading behaviours of particular sociological groups against their lived experience outside of the rarified space of dominant cultural production:

> Based on researching an all-female reading group in 'Smithton', [America] [Radway] observed an important difference between the continuation of a patriarchal hegemony in...genre romances...and a moment of resistance in the act of reading. The "resistance" here was in the act of the romance reader distancing herself, through the act of reading, from her obligations as wife, mother, carer—that is, from being secondary to someone else's needs. (Kiernan 2011)

This approach to studying writing foregrounds the reader's experience, as they actively (and subjectively) make meaning through reading. In contrast to Thompson's fascination with the book publishing elite, Janice Radway's project was founded on a democratising impulse. Radway's preoccupation with participation in the context of literature and publishing is a defining characteristic of her book *Reading the Romance*. For Radway, "The ethnographic turn began to have relevance for me when I began to engage simultaneously with the theoretical work on the reader developing within the literary critical community and the semiotic conceptions of the literary text" (Radway 1991, 4). She went on to say that *Reading the Romance* was "designed to investigate reading empirically so as to make 'accurate' statements about the historical and cultural meaning of literary production and consumption" (Ibid).

This foregrounding of the importance of "interpretative communities" is significant for writing culture in general, and publishing in particular, in terms of engaging with audiences. Tyson explains how one might apply the pedagogy of Reader-Response Criticism in the classroom: "As Bleich notes, one's announcement that one likes or dislikes a text, character, or passage is not enough to articulate taste. Rather, students must analyze the psychological pay-offs or costs the text creates for them and describe how these factors create their likes and dislikes" (Tyson 2006, 182). Reader-Response Criticism can be seen to enact a process of engagement that might usefully be applied to social media activity, since the reader is encouraged to interrogate their own response to the text before accepting their personal preferences, "likes" or "dislikes".

One of the main criticisms levelled at social media activity—and particularly Twitter—is that debates often become emotionally charged and irrational and preoccupied by intersecting subjectivities (Lorenz 2019). The Purdue Writing lab expands on this understanding, asserting that Reader-Response theory shares common ground with Barthes' suggestion in "The death of the author" that the (author)itarian figure in the text can be displaced (Purdue University n.d.). Both Barthes' reneging of the notion of a fixed meaning and the active application of Reader-Response techniques can be viewed as a prelude to the advent of digital criticism, online reviewing and curation, in which the experience of often unknown bloggers and influencers (the new cultural intermediaries) can become as significant (in terms of social media "likes" and sales) as the views of experts.

One such example can be found in an experiment in disruptive amateurism which reveals the problem of dispensing with gatekeepers. In 2018, a *Vice* magazine journalist tested the limits of influencing consumer behaviour on Tripadvisor by setting up a hoax restaurant called The Shed in Dulwich, London. Through a marketing campaign that included a multitude of fake reviews and by manufacturing an air of exclusivity by consistently turning away potential customers, The Shed briefly became the number one restaurant in London (according to Tripadvisor)—despite the fact that it didn't actually exist (Butler 2017). In this way, the promotional stunt revealed that without gatekeepers (in this case editors) monitoring the content on particular platforms, it is possible to subvert the ranking system with false-positive reviews. Applied to criticism, novelist Ben Wilson explains: "I feel like criticism is often published now on the basis of how many clicks it might get, rather than the nuance of the author"

(Wilson 2019). Wilson's comments allude to a significant issue in the production and dissemination of information in the public sphere, namely, the concurrent hype-based success of populist projects and the erosion of professional gatekeepers online.

CRITICS AND SOCIAL NETWORKS

The surfeit of digital content is therefore synonymous with the absence of gatekeepers and the growth of "amateur creativity" online. In "Amateur creativity: contemporary literature and the digital publishing scene", Aarthi Vadde asserts that: "Everybody's a critic...is a phrase often uttered in exasperation and with the implication that 'everybody' lacks expertise and authority, if not circumspection. This 'everybody,' in other words, is an amateur" (Vadde 2017, 27). Amateurism, with its connotations of uninformed opinions and enthusiasm, is part of a discourse that is often articulated as a means of putting clear water between generalists and specialists. This tension was also investigated by Reuters in 2014, when their research institute at the University of Oxford published a report titled "Anyone can be a critic: Is there still a need for professional arts and culture journalism in the digital age?" The report articulated the question that almost all publications must address now, namely: Why would readers pay for content when they can read what they want for free?

It is apparent that the role of reviewers has radically changed. Getting paid to write reviews, let alone attending literary lunches and flat-planning review pages, is an increasingly rarified role enjoyed by the few and challenged by the many new influencers, professional bloggers and free reviewers on the block. Literary critics, like many other arts reviewers, have been adversely affected by the decline of print sales and the growing avalanche of digital content. The quality press in the UK, for instance, has cut back on critical writing about the arts, with the *Independent on Sunday* dropping "The Critics" section in 2013 and The *Telegraph* halving its arts budget in 2008 and then cutting its head of arts role in 2016 (Sweney 2016).

CULTURAL ELITISM VERSUS RELATABLE READS

James Curran's enquiry into "Literary editors, social networks and cultural traditions" in 2000 exposed the structural inequalities and instinctive behaviour of literary editors which seems somewhat archaic in light of the shift towards data-driven decision making today. By combining quantitative data (content analysis) and qualitative data (interviews with literary editors), Curran was able to discern inconsistencies in terms of perceptions around reviewing culture (Curran 2000). His research showed that cultural intermediaries, and specifically book critics, tended to be male, Oxbridge educated, well connected and largely predisposed to reviewing books that mirrored their own cultural experience, network and interests. When he interviewed eleven literary editors from national newspapers and weekly periodicals, he discovered that a "stock response" was that "literary editors merely respond...to the external world" (Curran 2000, 216, cited in Kiernan 2011, 127). They deciphered a "pre-set agenda shaped by what readers are interested in, and what is being talked about" alongside a need to cover new works by important authors with established reputations and track records (Curran 2000, 216).

More confusingly—and this is the nub of Curran's findings—literary editors appeared to be unclear about what it was, exactly, that they did, despite simultaneously believing their roles to be well defined. Curran found that the rationales given for selecting particular titles were somewhat mystifying given that many critics "invoked a theory of predestination in which books were not chosen but chose themselves", while others "summoned an image of improvisation and randomness...governed by instinct and insight, without a clear pattern" (Curran 2000, 216; Kiernan 2011, 127). This rather vague sense of what literary editors do is quite different from the expectations of the form (of criticism) itself. Applied to Curran's privileged interviewees, the word "predestination" can be read as implying that the literary choices critics make are inevitable and should not be questioned. In this era of digital communication, the notion of predestination is at odds with the ideal of personal agency afforded through the Internet and also with the idea of a functioning meritocracy in which talent and effort are rewarded rather than wealth or social class (see Chap. 4 for further discussion on this topic).

Peter Stothard, chair of the Booker prize in 2012 and previously editor of both *The Times* and The *Times Literary Supplement*, seems to embody Curran's findings, at least in terms of his belief in the authority of the elite critic and in his unremitting view that blogs about books pose a threat to literary criticism (seen by him as a purveyor of difficult ideas to the general reader). His appointment to chair the Booker followed on from that of Stella Rimington, former director general of the M15, whom he distanced himself from, with reference to her ideal Booker submission being "readable" (Bloomgarden-Smoke 2012).[3]

In contrast to Rimington, Stothard's view appears to be that literature should do more than distract and delight the reader: "If we make the main criteria good, page-turning stories—if we prioritise unargued opinion over criticism—then I think literature will be harmed...Someone has to stand up for the role and the art of the critic, otherwise it will just be drowned—overwhelmed. And literature will be worse off" (Flood 2012). While Stothard's assertion sounds highfalutin, its twofold meaning is a useful anchor-point for this discussion. Firstly, his choice of words—"drowned—overwhelmed"—alludes to one of the primary challenges for writing culture in a digital age, which is to do with volume. As Kenneth Goldsmith surmises in *Uncreative Writing*, "Difficulty is now defined by quantity (too much to read) rather than fragmentation (too shattered to read)" (Goldsmith 2011, 12). Secondly, Stothard suggests that "Unargued opinion" is synonymous with "appreciation", a response pejoratively aligned to entertainment rather than high art, in all its forms.

While the tension between high culture and the assertion of value through the well-worn channels attributed to the connected and the elite seems to have changed little in more than a century in some quarters, in other, arguably more egalitarian communities, Stothard's views seem unreconstructed. Simon Savidge, reviewer and book blogger for Waterstones and at Savidge Reads: The Chronicles of a Book Addict, responded by saying that he found Stothard's views "disheartening...I think anyone who reads a lot, just by reading, has the ability to critique anything they read" (Savidge 2012).

CRITICISM VERSUS REVIEWING

Savidge's rebuff to Stothard is illuminating in that it alludes to the confusion between the taxonomies of criticism and reviewing. Critics usually have more cultural and symbolic capital, which is expressed through their expertise in the discipline they're passing judgement on and their network of contacts. In response to my survey question, "Is there still a need for professional arts and culture journalism in the digital age?" publisher Alison Jones said: "There's space for popular and professional

[3] See also Saha and van Lente on publisher's "comping" practices for more on this in Chap. 4.

opinion—good criticism is still worth reading, it's entertaining and informative in its own right" (Jones 2019). Sam Leith, journalist and author of *Write to the Point*, responded by saying that "I think there's a value in professional criticism—but it's silly to imagine it's under threat from the emergence of a wider critical community" (Leith 2019). Because cultural capital is what differentiates the every(wo)man reviewer from the critic, Leith's suggestion that it's "silly" to suggest that the former is a threat could be construed as denoting a belief in society's existing hierarchy, in which economic and educational status informs one's ability to contribute to the cultural conversation and, just as importantly, to be listened to.

Conclusion

The social, cultural and economic framework in which we find ourselves (or what Bourdieu refers to as Habitus) informs our ability to decipher and reproduce meaning, which is inevitably informed by educational and economic factors. As Bourdieu explains: "the apprehension and possession of cultural goods as symbolic goods...are possible only for those who hold the code making it possible to decipher them or, in other words, that the appropriation of symbolic goods presupposes the possession of the instruments of appropriation" (Bourdieu 2003, 64). This is perhaps why Leith is able to confidently dismiss the notion that the views of the masses are a threat to the critical status quo, since the class system in Britain, in which the ruling elite is predominantly upper middle class and Oxbridge educated, still dominates the pillars of democracy, namely, the legislature, executive and judiciary but also the media, which is what Curran revealed through his research project about critics nearly twenty years ago.

This chapter began by reflecting on how the role of cultural gatekeepers, and the language used to describe them, has changed. It has explored social networks in relation to the status inferred by social and economic capital and has concluded that user-generated reviews have significantly affected how literary culture is accessed. Underpinning this discussion is an enquiry into the residual tension between highbrow and popular contemporary culture, which Meredith Miller, in the opening quote to this chapter, suggests is a contributing factor in the "'democratic deficit' we are experiencing in the west" (Miller 2019) and which is discussed further in the chapters that follow.

REFERENCES

Bloomgarden-Smoke, Kara. 2012. British Literary Editor Bemoans Current State of Literary Criticism. *The Observer*, September 26. https://observer.com/2012/09/british-literary-editor-bemoans-current-state-of-literary-criticism/. Accessed 15 July 2020.

Bourdieu, Pierre. 2003. Cultural Reproduction and Social Reproduction. In *Culture: Critical Concepts in Sociology*, ed. Chris Jenks. London: Routledge.

Butler, Oobah. 2017. I Made My Shed the Top Rated Restaurant on TripAdvisor. *Vice*, December 6. https://www.vice.com/en_uk/article/434gqw/i-made-my-shed-the-top-rated-restaurant-on-tripadvisor. Accessed 20 June 2020.

Curran, James. 2000. Literary Editors, Social Networks and Cultural Tradition. In *Media Organizations in Society*, ed. James Curran. London: Arnold.

Flood, Alison 2012. Books bloggers are harming literature, warns Booker prize head judge. *The Guardian*, September 25. https://www.theguardian.com/books/2012/sep/25/books-bloggers-literature-booker-prize-stothard. Accessed 6 June 2021.

Goldsmith, Kenneth. 2011. *Uncreative Writing*. New York: Columbia University Press.

Hebdige, Dick. 1979. *Subculture: The Meaning of Style*. Abingdon-on-Thames: Routledge.

Houser, Heather. 2020. *Infowhelm: Environmental Art and Literature in an Age of Data*. New York: Columbia University Press.

Jones, Alison. 2019. This quote is from an online survey I ran between January and March 2019 (See Appendix).

Kennedy, Krista. 2016. *Textual Curation: Authorship, Agency, and Technology in Wikipedia and Chamber's Cyclopedia*. Columbia: University of South Carolina Press.

Kiernan, Anna. 2011. The Growth of Reading Groups as a Feminine Leisure Pursuit: Cultural Democracy or Dumbing Down? In *From Salons to Cyberspace: Readings of Reading Communities*, ed. Denel Rehberg. London: Palgrave.

La Force, Thessaly. 2012. *My Ideal Bookshelf*. London: Little, Brown.

Leith, Sam. 2019. This quote is from an online survey I ran between January and March 2019 (See Appendix).

Lorenz, Taylor. 2019. It's Impossible to Follow a Conversation on Twitter. *The Atlantic*, February 15. https://www.theatlantic.com/technology/archive/2019/02/its-impossible-follow-conversation-twitter/582907/. Accessed 30 Mar 2019.

Miller, Meredith. 2019. Online Survey Conducted by the Author (See Appendix).

Mullan, Eileen. 2011. What Is Content Curation? *Econtent Magazine*, November 30. http://www.econtentmag.com/Articles/Resources/Defining-EContent/What-is-Content-Curation-79167.htm. Accessed 30 June 2019.

Purdue University. n.d. Reader-Response Criticism. Purdue Writing Lab. https://owl.purdue.edu/owl/subject_specific_writing/writing_in... Accessed 30 Mar 2019.

Radway, Janice. 1991. *Reading the Romance: Women, Patriarchy and Popular Culture.* Chapel Hill: University of North Carolina Press.

Ritvo, Harriet. 1998. *The Platypus and the Mermaid: And Other Figments of the Classifying Imagination.* Cambridge, MA: Harvard University Press.

Savidge, Simon. 2012. Defending Book Blogging. *Savidge Reads* (Blog). September 26. https://savidgereads.wordpress.com/2012/09/26/defending-book-blogging/

Sweney, Mark. 2016. Deputy Editor and Other Top Staff Exit in Newsroom Cull. *Telegraph*, May 24. https://www.theguardian.com/media/2016/may/24/telegraph-deputy-editor-newsroom-cull. Accessed 30 June 2019.

Thompson, John B. 2010. *Merchants of Culture: The Publishing Business in the Twenty-First Century.* Cambridge: Polity.

Tyson, Lois. 2006. *Critical Theory Today: A User-Friendly Guide.* New York: Routledge. https://www.academia.edu/12530113/Critical_Theory_Today_by_Lois_Tyson

University of California, Los Angeles. n.d.. From the Digital Humanities Manifesto 2.0. UCLA. http://manifesto.humanities.ucla.edu/. Accessed 30 Mar 2019.

Vadde, Aarthi. 2017. Amateur Creativity: Contemporary Literature and the Digital Publishing Scene. *New Literary History* 48 (1 Winter): 27–51, 194. https://doi.org/10.1353/nlh.2017.0001.

Wilcox, Claire. 2020. *Patch Work: A Life Amongst Clothes.* London: Bloomsbury.

Wilson, Ben. 2019. This Quote Is from an Online Survey I Ran Between January and March 2019 (See Appendix).

CHAPTER 4

Diversity, Representation and Innovation in Online Literary Promotion

It does seem that there's a big problem with what and whose stories are being commissioned, funded, marketed, publicised and, ultimately, read. The industry is rife with exclusion and marginalisation, which will take a long time to rectify. (Zoë King, 2021)[1]

The previous chapter discussed the changing role of critics and curators in the digital age. Twenty years after Professor James Curran published "Literary Editors, Social Networks and Cultural Tradition" (2000), fellow Goldsmiths academics Dr. Anamik Saha and Dr. Sandra van Lente revealed ongoing systemic inequalities within the literary industries, with their "Rethinking 'Diversity' in Publishing" report (2020). While Curran's research disclosed gender- and class-based inequities among literary gate-keepers, "Rethinking 'Diversity'" examines the ways in which writers of colour are published. Conducted by Goldsmiths University in partnership with *The Bookseller* magazine and Spread the Word and funded by the Arts and Humanities Research Council, the report draws on qualitative interviews with 113 publishing professionals "to show how woefully lacking the industry still is in acquiring, publishing, promoting and selling work by writers of colour" (Howdle 2021). Both publications draw on

---

[1] Zoë King was assistant publisher for The Tilt, which was published by The Literary Platform. The Tilt "calls for a shift in the industry story" and showcases the "change that each contributor wants to see enacted in publishing and the literary industries" (King 2021).

© The Author(s), under exclusive license to Springer Nature Switzerland AG 2021
A. Kiernan, *Writing Cultures and Literary Media*, New Directions in Book History, https://doi.org/10.1007/978-3-030-75081-7_4

interviews with industry professionals and it is interesting to note prevailing similarities in both the tone and content of industry insiders over a twenty-year period. This chapter draws on postcolonial theory to take an intersectional approach to discussing recurring modes of discrimination and privilege within the literary industries. It then goes on to highlight some of the ways in which digital communication and online communities present opportunities for countering structural inequalities in terms of promoting the work of underrepresented writers.

Saha and van Lente suggest that "'diversity', when it is understood as giving special affordances to writers of colour, is seen as potentially undermining publishing's meritocratic foundations" (Saha and van Lente 2020, 19). Many publishers' implicit rejection of diversity is therefore based on an old-fashioned belief that "if it's good we will publish it" (Saha and van Lente 2020, 19). In other words, there is an unspoken belief that the diversity agenda is at odds with the meritocratic system of narrative selection (both within commissioning and hiring practices). Such assessments are largely informed by the publisher, editor or agents' own experiences and world view, which can be seen to implicitly limit the definition of what is "good", in terms of its relation to books they have read previously, which may have had an impact on critics, the canon and the marketplace. Saha and van Lente's report usefully unpicks the concept of "quality", which is sometimes intuitively applied by publishing professionals:

> In an industry that is dominated by the white middle-classes, many of whom attended Russell Group universities, notions of 'quality' are shaped by a very particular experience and education, based on a canon that in recent times has been questioned for its Eurocentric view of the world. (Saha and van Lente 2020, 19)

CULTURE AND IMPERIALISM

The qualitative concept of "quality" is ideologically loaded, particularly when considered in the context of experience, education and literature, since it has historical foundations in the project of culture and imperialism. As Edward Said suggested in his book *Culture and Imperialism*, the word culture (lower case) denotes anthropological relevances (such as everyday life experiences and education), while the capitalised form of Culture can be seen to signify the arts. These two understandings of the idea of culture are interlinked and, within the imperialist project of the nineteenth century, culture and Culture were interdependent, particularly when considered in the context of Western literary production, of which the novel is the most comprehensive example. Said explains:

> I am not trying to say that the novel—or the culture in the broad sense—'caused' imperialism, but that the novel, as a cultural artefact of bourgeois society, and imperialism are unthinkable without each other... imperialism and the novel fortified each other to such a degree that it is impossible... to read one without in some way dealing with the other. (Said 1994, 84)

That the novel form was traditionally bound up in the project of empire poses challenges for the writer and publisher alike. It is therefore helpful to consider the historical specificity of cultural production when negotiating the issue of diversity in publishing and to review the limits of a meritocratic mindset, given the limitations, in terms of social access to the means of production, for underrepresented writers. This perspective is particularly relevant in investigating the conditions of production in contemporary trade publishing.

This dilemma has been played out in London novels for decades, from Zadie Smith's *White Teeth* (2000) to Bernardine Evaristo's *Girl, Woman, Other* (2019), in which Yazz, one of the twelve black British female protagonists, observes that "privilege is about context and circumstance" (Evaristo 2019, 72). In *White Teeth*, the narrator explains that the (white) family, the Chalferns, demonstrate a guiding belief in the authority of their intellectual ancestry by saying that "In the Chalfern lexicon the middle classes were the inheritors of the enlightenment, the creators of the welfare state, the intellectual elite and the source of all culture" (Smith 2000, 372). In the same way that Marcus Chalfern, an eminent scientist, authenticates his hypothesis on life through studying recombinant DNA technology, so too the Chalferns view their own existence as being logical, inevitable and therefore superior.

Studies of the contemporary publishing industry often exist within a Eurocentric or Anglo-American frame of reference (as does this one) (Wallis 2016). In *Merchants of Culture*, for instance, John B. Thompson investigates the structures, communities and institutions that characterise trade publishing and explains his approach to the study of literary culture thus:

> I have studied this world in the way that an anthropologist would study the practices of a tribe inhabiting some remote island in the South Pacific, only in this case the tribe lives and works, for the most part, in a small section of an island squeezed between...New York...and London. (Thompson 2010, vii)

Thompson's methodology connects the study of writing culture and the people who comprise that culture, through a socio-anthropological perspective, casually objectifying "a tribe" on "some remote island". This othering tendency should not be overlooked, since it can be read as reflecting a similar tendency within the publishing "tribe" that Thompson investigates, in his exploration of the Anglo-American trade publishing business in the twenty-first century. Peter McLarensuggested in "White Terror and Oppositional Agency: Towards a CriticalMulticulturalism" that, in order to understand such pre-eminent Westernperceptions of culture, the conditions of its production should be interrogated, asmust the culture of whiteness itself" (McLaren 1994, 59). This perspective isparticularly relevant in investigating both the conditions of production incontemporary trade publishing, and also perceptions around the circulation ofcultural value, such as Thompson's above. As Sarah Brouillette explains in *Postcolonial Writers in theGlobal Literary Marketplace*, valueis determined in relation to "the specific interconnections between the content ofliterary work and the circuits through which texts pass as they are produced and consumed" (Brouillette 2007, 176–177).

Opening Up the Narrative

Through their report on diversity, Saha and van Lente shared the findings from their investigation into the conditions of production within publishing and the literary industries. The report has catalysed a shift in how diversity, particularly in relation to writers of colour, and representations thereof, is perceived by industry insiders. The culture of whiteness is scrutinised throughout the Goldsmiths report and specifically in terms of unspoken expectations of "otherness" in the "Conforming to Whiteness" section. Many "BAME" respondents felt creatively inhibited by what they perceived to be a particular set of narrative expectations from prospective publishers and felt that "in order to get a publishing deal they had to fulfil certain expectations of what white, middle-class editors want" (Saha and van Lente 2020, 14). This stems in part from "comping", which means comparing submissions with comparable books in order to assess potential audiences and sales. Saha and van Lente go on to quote from an interview which states that "I think a lot of white editors were like 'We thought you were giving us this immigrant narrative'" (Ibid). This view is also apparent in Claire Squires' chapter "Too Much Rushdie, Not Enough Romance?:

The UK Publishing Industry and BME (Black Minority Ethnic) Readership". Squires notes that while "all agents in the circuit begin as readers...their varying positions...combine to effectuate patterns of literary and demographic stereotyping" (Squires 2012, 106). In "Arts, Media and Ethnic Inequalities", Malik and Shankley suggest that because of this self-perpetuating bias, BAME communities "are required to 'act white'— to behave in a certain manner to be included and accepted...they are often excluded from the knowledge and/ or expected behaviours that are needed for entry" (Malik and Shankley 2020, 173). In the findings section of the Goldsmiths report, Saha and van Lente reveal a central obstruction to change, which is that of the perceived homogenous audience for books, the prerequisite for which is privilege, of "context and circumstance" (Evaristo 2019, 72):

> The core audience for publishers is white and middle-class. The whole industry is essentially set up to cater for this one audience. This affects how writers of colour and their books are treated, which are either whitewashed or exoticised in order to appeal to this segment. (Saha and van Lente 2020, 4)

A literary manifestation of this issue can again be found in Smith's *White Teeth*, during a classroom debate about Shakespeare's sonnet "My Mistress' Eyes Are Nothing Like the Sun", in which Irie's English teacher, Mrs. Roody, has the following conversation with Irie (the protagonist) (Smith 2000, 234–5):

> "Have you anything to say about the sonnets?"
> "Yes."
> "What?"
> "Is she black?"
> "Is who black?"
> "The dark lady."
> "No dear, she's dark. She's not black in the modern sense. There weren't any...well Afro-Carri-bee-yans in England at that time, dear."

Mrs. Roody's negative (and inaccurate) response to Irie's suggestion that the "dark lady" was black exposes misconceptions based on assumptions pertaining to the construction of cultural value and identity. In *Playing in the Dark: Whiteness and the Literary Imagination*, Toni Morrison discusses the ways in which the Great Literary Tradition, which largely ignores any black presence, should be re-read. Irie's suggestion echoes Toni Morrison's belief in the importance of reinscribing literary texts with readings which are sensitive to a latent black presence but her contribution is dismissed by her teacher, thereby revealing structural inequalities within both educational and literary discourses. The exclusivity of such discourses can be seen to contribute to a sense of social and cultural exclusion, with this fictional example also finding form in recent research, such as The Literacy Trust's report on diversity. The report revealed that, based on responses from 60,000 young readers, 33% felt unrepresented "with an even worse picture among poorer and minority ethnic readers" (Flood 2020).

Unsurprisingly, there is a correlation between educational experiences, representations in literature and professional aspirations, each of which forms a connecting thread within a value chain that exists, as it were, outside of the norms associated with the accumulation of cultural capital espoused by Thompson in *Merchants of Culture*. A case in point is *The Other Black Girl* (2021) by Zakiya Dalila Harris, which addresses the lack of diversity within the publishing industry through a fictional account of editorial assistant Nella Rogers' experience of being the only black employee at Wagner Books. This unsettling thriller presents an astute social satire about the limitations of a monocultural industry. In her reflective review of the novel in *The Bookseller* magazine, Silé Edwards, an agent at Mushens Entertainment, says that "The novel is a window into what it is to survive as the only Black girl in a predominantly white space" (Edwards 2020). Edwards goes on to reflect on her own experiences of working in publishing, stating that: "As a black woman especially, you are ever conscious of appearing angry or being accused of not making enough of an effort to fit into the company culture" (Edwards 2020). Edwards' acknowledgement of the apparent need to suppress emotional expression as part of a conscious strategy to appear more likeable (and therefore promotable) can be read as an outcome of cultural assimilation.

Narratives of assimilation (often expressed as the need to fit in) are therefore evident both in fictional representations of publishing and in the emergent counter-narratives which explicitly reject assimilatory expectations. *Taking Up Space: The Black Girl's Manifesto for Change* (2019) begins with "A Letter to My Fresher Self", which includes insights such as "You will have supervisors who call you defensive and angry and who will project their own prejudiced stereotypes onto you as you walk into the room" (Kwakye and Ogunbiyi 2019, 1). Elizabeth Uviebinené and Yomi Adegoke, co-authors of *Slay in Your Lane: The Black Girl's Bible*, echo this sentiment, explaining that while women are encouraged to "lean in" in the workplace, "when you're a black woman, such behaviour also comes with stereotypes of being aggressive, angry and unco-operative" (Onwuemezi 2018).

Slay in Your Lane was one of Fourth Estate's lead titles in 2018 and was commissioned following a nine-publisher auction. The premise for the book, and the promotional campaign, was to celebrate and amplify "the voices and visibility of trailblazing black British women". The project consciously rejected the assumed audience that so many publishers target through their lists[2] and, as such, was agenda-setting, not only in terms of its subject matter but also in terms of the success of its promotional campaign. Adegoke and Uviebinené drew on an "army of influencers" (including June Sarpong, Denise Lewis, Dawn Butler and Funke Abimbola) to promote the project and the book (Onwuemezi 2018). As content producers and journalists with more than 20,000 followers between them on Twitter, the authors engaged with audiences on social media in creative ways that an in-house marketing campaign might have struggled to reach, let alone appeal to. The book's success therefore hinged on the authors' energy and ability to influence—and draw on relevant influencers—to promote their work. *Slay in Your Lane* (2018) has become a reference point for publishers set on diversifying their lists and "comping" tried-and-tested publishing success stories. The success of this title was significant for the industry in that it opened up publishing possibilities by demonstrating that strategic social media campaigns have the potential to convert untapped creative communities into superfans, thereby illuminating commercial opportunities (Lovell 2014).

Taking Up Space

As Saha and van Lente (2020) suggest, via a quote from a 'BAME' respondent in the concluding pages of their report:[3]

> The digital space now gives us a great opportunity to really experiment and try new things, because we can now target more audiences. We've got the tools to do that and start through data these social media companies supply

---

[2] Saha and van Lente explain in their report that: "The idea of the core reader as a white, middle-class older woman (sardonically referred to as 'Susan' by several of our respondents) remains dominant" (Saha and van Lente 2020, 14).

[3] The term BAME is problematic because, "like 'black' and 'coloured' before it, [it]was doomed to fail because it's impossible to distill centuries of history and culture into a handy acronym." (Mistlin 2021)

now. We can identify who is the target market, what's their behaviour and how we connect with them...we can start talking to them, start engaging with them, without worrying about a buyer at Tesco or a buyer at Asda. (Saha and van Lente 2020, 32)

While Saha and van Lente observe the need for more creative promotional strategies, their warning that "Genuine relationships need to be built with these new media so that such an engagement does not feel opportunistic" (Saha and van Lente 2020, 36) invites further reflection. Marketing tactics on social media are often necessarily opportunistic in that they thrive on real-time conversations in order to promote engagement. The risk is perhaps more that the success of these publications seems to depend on the authors' networks and commitment to being vocal about their books. The challenge for publishers' publicity departments is to be able to build capacity (in terms of the representative diversity of their staff) in order to generate promotional strategies that serve the authors rather than simply following their lead online.

Yomi Adegoke and Elizabeth Uviebinené are digital-first communicators and influencers who, like Ore Ogunbiyi and Chelsea Kwakye, are committed to speaking up, despite—and also to some extent because of—the prejudices they have experienced as "opinionated" women. This presents a conundrum: How much of the promotional momentum should be contingent on the authors' drive and, if the success of emerging writers of colour is dependent on their social media profile, to what extent is the author expected to conform to the constraint of seeming to be "likeable"?

The Problem of Likeable Characters

As Saha and van Lente's research shows, writers of colour are especially marginalised in terms of structural conditions of production, but, despite these structural conditions, the growing appeal of author-led campaigns (such as Adegoke and Uviebinené's above) has created an opening in the publishing praxis. In terms of reception, understood here as the way that readers and critics respond to the work, a significant tension persists, with regard to audience expectations around homogenised characters. Daniel Allington's study, "'Power to the reader' or 'degradation of literary taste'? Professional critics and Amazon customers as reviewers of *The Inheritance of Loss*", explores representation and the problem of complexity (in terms of characters and plot) in relation to postcolonial fiction, through research that draws out cultural differences manifest in the contrast between online reader reviews and the views of literary critics.

Drawing on responses to Kiran Desai's novel *The Inheritance of Loss* (2008), which won the Man Booker Prize and the National Book Critics Circle Award for Fiction, Allington found that reviews for the book on Amazon were mixed. In contrast, qualitative analysis of the largely homogenous group of professional reviewers' reviews was largely positive. His research showed that customer reviews were more likely to criticise the novel for its characters and less likely to discuss its political themes (Allington 2016). The dismissive stance towards the vicissitudes of cultural difference are glossed over in the Amazon reviews, in favour of focusing on characters, the story arc and whether the work is easy to relate to or not. By emphasising the "likeability" of key characters, customer reviews of Desai's novel tended to celebrate the moment of emotional connection between characters, as opposed to engaging with more complex questions raised through discussions of politics and identity, moral ambiguity and experiments with form—just some of the characteristics which differentiate literary fiction from genre fiction. Likeability infers relatability which, applied in this way, can be seen to be reductionist in terms of diversity of form and content. However, the circulation of cultural value remains influenced by critical discourse (or the lack thereof) despite the growth of audience-generated reviews and commentaries, and this can be seen to generate a misleading sense of what the literary industries could and should be showcasing and sharing in order to diversify audiences and generate new understandings of what "quality" and cultural value look like.

As Saha and van Lente have shown, diversifying the circulation of cultural value within the literary industries must be a root and branch endeavour. The final example in this chapter therefore relates to the Booker Prize, "The leading literary award in the English speaking world", an annual event that promotes the circulation of both cultural and economic value (English 2008). When the judges jointly awarded Bernardine Evaristo and Margaret Atwood in 2019 they set two precedents: the first being that Evaristo was the first female writer of colour to receive the award; the second being that she received only half of the award (and therefore only half of the financial reward). In terms of the circulation of cultural value, one connotation seemed to be that the value of Evaristo's literary contribution had been halved. Despite reports from the Booker judges that the verdict was unanimous, the media's reaction to the fallout from the decision was largely negative (Wagner 2019; Flood 2019), and, in the case of Sunny Singh, incandescent.

In her article in *gal-dem* (a new media company committed to sharing the perspectives of women and non-binary people of colour) Singh said: "Apparently, the chair of judges, Peter Florence 'refused to give way' on choosing a single winner—a rather telling statement given that he was chairing a jury made up of four women, including two women of colour. He seemingly demanded and was able to push through a decision flouting the prize's own rules" (Singh 2019). Singh, who co-founded the Jhalak Prize for the Book of the Year by a Writer of Colour in 2016, strongly believed that Evaristo should have won the award outright. But it was the reaction to Evaristo's rallying Tweet that signalled a tipping point in terms of public opinion and the post-prize discourse. Evaristo tweeted: "The @ BBC described me yesterday as 'another author' apropos @TheBookerPrizes 2019. How quickly & casually they have removed my name from history—the first black woman to win it. This is what we've always been up against, folks". Reweeted almost 10,000 times, the Tweet was certainly forthright but also indisputably "likeable": it garnered more than 13,700 Likes.

Evaristo's "another author" tweet is just one example of how digital communication offers up opportunities for countering structural inequalities in terms of promoting the work of underrepresented writers. Saha and van Lente's report concludes that "Social media has enabled audiences to publicly talk back to publishers in a way that was never the case before, to the extent they can make or break books" (Saha and van Lente 2020, 34). Publishers are well aware of this shift, and the focus on digital at the end of the report signifies an entrenched behaviour within the literary industries to add the digital bit on at the end, as it were, rather than recognising, as Adegoke and Uviebinené do, that social media is central to the publishing and promotional campaign from conception to publication.

CONCLUSION

To conclude, this chapter has focused on contemporary case studies which illuminate recurring issues of representation within the literary industries, with regard to writers of colour. It has also highlighted some of the positive ways in which publishing norms are being challenged by influencers, and specifically female writers of colour, online. The hypervigilance around acceptable normative emotional discourse is significant within both the academy and the publishing industry, in that it contains echoes of the kind of limiting binary oppositions that have historically posited women and people of colour as being less rational, thereby less civilised and therefore less worthy of autonomy and power than their male counterparts (McLaren 1994, 55).[4] And so to conclude this chapter, I would suggest that the significance of social media (and Twitter in particular), in terms of agenda-setting and holding the mainstream media to account, is evident both in the success of authors such as Adegoke and Uviebinené and in the fallout from industry anomalies such as the Booker Prize in 2019. These cultural shifts signal a need for publishers to be more creative in their promotional strategies: "They need to develop a stronger awareness of the new media channels beyond the mainstream that are reaching previously neglected audiences" (Saha and van Lente 2020, 36). Challenging the lack of diversity in the field is not only a pressing social and cultural concern, but, as the examples in this chapter have attempted to show, also presents a commercial opportunity for publishers, in terms of working with overlooked authors and marketing to new audiences.

References

Adegoke, Yomi, and Uviebinené, Elizabeth. 2018. *Slay in Your Lane: The Black Girl Bible*. London: Fourth Estate.

Allington, Daniel. 2016. "Power to the Reader" or "Degradation of Literary Taste"? Professional Critics and Amazon Customers as Reviewers of the Inheritance of Loss. *Language and Literature* 25 (3): 254–278. https://doi.org/10.1177/0963947016652789.

Brouillette, Sarah. 2007. *Postcolonial Writers in the Global Literary Marketplace*. Houndmills: Palgrave Macmillan.

Curran, James. 2000. Literary Editors, Social Networks and Cultural Tradition. In *Media Organizations in Society*, ed. James Curran. London: Arnold.

Desai, Kiran. 2008. *The Inheritance of Loss*. London: Penguin.

Edwards, Silé. 2020. The Only Black Girl. *Bookseller*, December 24. https://www.thebookseller.com/blogs/only-black-girl-1231065. Accessed 14 Jan 2021.

English, James F. 2008. *The Economy of Prestige: Prizes, Awards, and the Circulation of Cultural Value*. Cambridge: Harvard University Press.

---

[4] "Western language and thought are constructed as a system of differences organized…as binary oppositions—white/black, good/bad, normal/deviant, etc.—with the primary term being privileged and designated as the defining terms or the norm of cultural meaning" (McLaren 1994, 55).

Evaristo, Bernardine. 2019. *Girl, Woman, Other*. London: Penguin.

Flood, Alison. 2019. Backlash After Booker Awards Prize to Two Authors. *The Guardian*, October 15. https://www.theguardian.com/books/2019/oct/15/bernardine-evaristo-margaret-atwood-share-booker-prize-award. Accessed 20 Jan 2021.

———. 2020. A Third of UK Children Do Not See Themselves Reflected in Books, Finds Survey. *The Guardian*, December 2. https://www.theguardian.com/books/2020/dec/02/third-of-uk-children-do-not-see-themselves-reflected-in-books-national-literary-trust-survey. Accessed 20 Jan 2021.

Dalila Harris, Zakiya. 2021. *The Other Black Girl: A Novel*. London: Bloomsbury.

Howdle, Clare. 2021. Interview with Sunny Singh. *The Tilt*. Falmouth: The Literary Platform.

———, ed. 2015. Writing the Future: Black and Asian Writers and Publishers in the UK Marketplace. www.spreadtheword.org.uk/writing-the-future/. Accessed 5 Jan 2021.

King, Zoë. 2021. *The Tilt*. Falmouth: The Lit Platform.

Kwakye, Chelsea, and Ogunbiyi, Ore. 2019. *Taking Up Space: The Black Girl's Manifesto*. London: Merky Books.

Lovell, Nicholas. 2014. *The Curve: Turning Followers into Superfans*. London: Penguin.

Malik, Sarita, and Shankley, William. 2020. Arts, Media and Ethnic Inequalities. In *Ethnicity and Race in the UK: State of the Nation*, ed. Shankley, William, et al., 1st ed., 167–188. Bristol/Chicago: Bristol University Press JSTOR. www.jstor.org/stable/j.ctv14t47tm.14. Accessed 9 Nov 2020.

McLaren, Peter. 1994. White Terror and Oppositional Agency: Towards a Critical Multiculturalism. In *Multiculturalism: A Critical Reader*, ed. D.T. Goldberg. London: Blackwell.

Mistlin, A. 2021. So the Term BAME Has Had Its Day. But What Should Replace It? *The Guardian*, April 8. https://www.theguardian.com/commentisfree/2021/apr/08/bame-britain-ethnic-minorities-acronym. Accessed 10 May 2021.

Morrison, Toni. 1992. *Playing in the Dark: Whiteness and the Literary Imagination*. Cambridge: Harvard University Press.

Onwuemezi, Natasha. 2018. Just Because Something Is by Black Women and About Black Women, That Doesn't Mean That It Can't Be Mainstream. *Bookseller*, June 16. https://www.thebookseller.com/profile/yomi-adegoke-elizabeth-uviebinen-just-because-something-black-women-and-about-black-women. Accessed 15 Jan 2021.

Saha, Anamik, and van Lente, Sandra. 2020. *Rethinking 'Diversity' in Publishing*. Project Report. London: Goldsmiths Press.

Said, W. Edward. 1994. *Culture and Imperialism*. London: Vintage.

Singh, Sunny. 2019. As the First Black Woman to Win the Booker Prize, Bernardine Evaristo Deserved to Win Alone. *Gal-dem*, October 15. https://gal-dem. com/as-the-first-black-woman-to-win-the-booker-prize-bernardine-evaristo-deserved-to-win-alone/. Accessed 30 Jan 2021.

Smith, Zadie. 2000. *White Teeth*. London: Penguin.

Squires, Claire. 2012. Too Much Rushdie, Not Enough Romance?: The UK Publishing Industry and BME (Black Minority Ethnic) Readership. In *Postcolonial Audiences: Readers, Viewers and Reception*, ed. Bethan Benwell, James Procter, and Gemma Robinson. New York: Routledge.

Wagner, Erica. 2019. The Booker Judges Reflect an Unhealthy Disregard for the Rules. *The Financial Times*, October 18. https://www.ft.com/content/63553614-f0da-11e9-a55a-30afa498db1b. Accessed 25 Jan 2021.

Wallis, Kate. 2016. How Books Matter: Kwani Trust, Farafina, Cassava Republic Press and the Medium of Print. In *Wasafiri*, ed. Ruth Bush and Madhu Krishnan. Vol. 31, 2016 – Issue 4: Print Activism in Twenty-First Century Africa. November 24. https://www.tandfonline.com/doi/full/10.1080/02690055.2016.1220698 Accessed 25 Jan 2021.

CHAPTER 5

Instagram, Poetry and the Cult of the Amateur

The brand is in a sense a further text, as much as the author is also in a constant process of authoring themselves. (Jack Underwood 2019)

In an article in the *New Yorker* in 2013, Thomas Beller asked the epistemological question, "Does a thought need to be shared to exist?" (Beller 2013; Oates 2012). Permutations of this question have resonated within literary circles (often via tweets) since online engagement became a seemingly necessary output for aspiring authors. Beller pointed out that "Most great writers could, if they wanted to, be very good at Twitter, because it is a medium of words and also of form" is a challenge of sorts but is also a persuasive leap of faith, as is his portent that succumbing (to social media) merely offers the illusion of authenticity at the cost of complexity: "We live in a transparent age, and yet there is much of value that happens in the opaque quarters of our own ambivalent minds" (Beller 2013). Ambivalence, a prerequisite for the kind of moral ambiguity that has historically helped to form a definition of literature, is often absent from interactions on Twitter and Instagram. Nevertheless, tweets by distinguished novelists such as Bernardine Evaristo and Margaret Atwood, and Instagram posts by so-called Instapoets such as Rupi Kaur to Hollie McNish, are consumed and shared enthusiastically by their fans and foes, with both positions delivering a remarkably similar outcome, namely, to attract attention to the authors and to the issues in question.

A. Kiernan, *Writing Cultures and Literary Media*, New Directions in Book History, https://doi.org/10.1007/978-3-030-75081-7_5

This chapter reflects on the function and form of Instapoetry, and the benefits (and limitations) of instantaneous publication, in contrast to the cultural considerations and processes that have historically informed the production and publication of poetry. It begins by considering the kinds of establishment poets who dominated the field at the start of the twenty-first century in the UK, in comparison to some of the most popular (insta) poets today. The characteristics of both the figure of the poet and the format or platform upon which poetry is (most often) engaged with have shifted. This shift is evident in both the diverse backgrounds and entrepreneurial attitudes of contemporary Instapoets, many of whom acknowledge their personal brand as a contributing factor in their commercial success. Sales figures for some of the best-known Instapoets have served to buoy the market, with poet and scholar Timothy Yu noting that, "In the mainstream press, the primary theme has been 'how Instagram saved poetry'" (Yu 2019). The shift is also evident in the mode of address (from detached and formal to immediate and relatable) and the form of the poetry being published.

In a blog post on the Poetry Foundation website titled "Instagram Poetry and Our Poetry Worlds", Yu expands his understanding of the etymology of the term poetry by reframing it to include not only the written and the spoken word but also "born digital" poetry that is shared through Instagram (Yu 2019). Acknowledging the latter as a discrete category reduces the need to compare Instapoetry unfavourably to poetry produced in line with formal structures and cadences within the academy (so with a focus on "craft") or with poetry that is written to be performed. Yu asserts the need for a renewed understanding of the field, in which Instapoetry is delineated from poetry written for "the page" or "the stage" (Yu 2019). In this way, Yu seems to be perched firmly on the fence between three fields: the raw emotion, energy and flow of live literature; the quietly intellectual space of traditional poetry and the entrepreneurial world of 24/7 Instapoetry production.

The Pre-digital Poetry Landscape

Twenty years ago, poetry was largely made up of the first two fields referred to above, namely, verse intended for the page or stage. At that time, research undertaken by Arts Council England (ACE) revealed that there was "an enormous gulf" between bestsellers, heavily promoted by their publishers, and other titles (cited in Ezard, 2000). After the United

Kingdom Net Book Agreement (NBA), which had been in place since 1899, began to collapse in 1994, large bookselling chains were able to reduce book prices. A price-fixing deal between British publishers and booksellers, the NBA meant that booksellers could stock a wide range of stock because the resale price allowed publishers to set a "net price" for the book. The demise of the NBA contributed to a more laissez faire culture in which marketing books and bookselling have been weighted in favour of books that can be bought at high volume for large discounts, such as mainstream bestsellers. This is in contrast to the small print runs with low discounts that are characteristic of poetry publishing, where only a handful of authors generate significant sales.

In the year 2000, the poetry market in the UK was dominated by erstwhile establishment figures: books by former laureate Ted Hughes sold 172,174 copies, giving him 49% of the market. Nobel laureate Seamus Heaney sold 34,690 books (just under 10%). In third place was former poet laureate Carol Ann Duffy, whose work sold 22,364 copies (6.3%) (Ezard 2000). The ACE report was released at a pre-digital turning point, in terms of access to audiences. Facebook, Instagram and Twitter didn't exist and the supermarkets were the designated threat at the time, in terms of their influence on homogenising publishing outputs (Squires 2007, 31). At that time, poets didn't have the necessary platforms at their fingertips for the shadow-work of self-promotion. That content is synchronously produced and consumed through iterative, highly responsive online communities is integral to the success of the most popular Instapoets today. It is in this context that the book sales of those under discussion in this chapter—many of whom are still early-career poets—seem worthy of note. As *The Bookseller* magazine revealed, Holly McNish's books sold 20,715 copies, Rupi Kaur 183,044 and Kate Tempest 67,465 copies (including her debut novel) by January 2018—a sobering quantitative comparison with the bestselling poets of twenty years ago (Wood 2018). In *The Adaptation Industry: The Cultural Economy of Contemporary Literary Adaptation*, Simone Murray describes this in Bourdieusian terms as the "loser wins" phenomenon, in which "the less successful an artwork is in market terms the more it accumulates cultural esteem, and vice versa" (Murray 2012, 19). The commercial success that some Instapoets enjoy takes place without the permission, as it were, of traditional gatekeepers, which has caused consternation among some critics.

THE NOBLE AMATEUR

While poetry has historically been infused with emotion, social media in general, and Instapoetry in particular, excel at relatability. As the *New York Times* put it, "Relatability is the chief psychological lubricant that glides you thoughtlessly down the curated, endless scroll of your feed" (Larson 2019). But "relatable" feeds, whether on platforms such as Facebook, Instagram or Twitter, can also feed a gnawing sense of alienation, in which the reader wonders why their world isn't quite so "shareable". Little wonder, then, that research undertaken at Stanford and New York Universities revealed that actions such as deleting Facebook accounts (and thereby negating the pressure of insidious consumerism online) can make you happier (O'Neil 2019; Soat 2015). The psychological implications of sharing our emotions online are not yet fully understood, but it is becoming increasingly apparent that imbibing the illusion of happiness on social media can lead to distorted expectations of our own experience of the world.

The sense of dis-ease at the notion of 'relatable' poetry being included within the literary canon may have been a contributing factor in leading British poetry periodical *PN Review* publishing an article by poet Rebecca Watts titled "The cult of the noble amateur" (Watts 2018). The thrust of the piece was that "amateur poets" publishing on social media were undermining poetry as an art form (Watts 2018). Watts' polemic begins with the perceived tensions between popular and highbrow literary culture: "I refer to the rise of a cohort of young female poets who are currently being lauded by the poetic establishment for their 'honesty' and 'accessibility'—buzzwords for the open denigration of intellectual engagement and rejection of craft that characterises their work" (Watts 2018). The article analyses several poems through a critical literary lens. Watts' assertion that "the current culture of reception [that focuses] on the author not the work" reveals a concern, which is widely held (but not necessarily widely shared) by writers (Watts 2018).

Watts cites T. S. Eliot in her piece, which situates her discussion within the established literary and critical canon. In *The Sacred Wood*, Eliot wrote that, "the poet has, not a 'personality' to express, but a particular medium, which is only a medium and not a personality" (Eliot 1982, 41). Eliot's view contrasts with the prevailing politics of identity, which are at the heart of the work of the most successful (commercially speaking) poets working now, from Hera Lindsay Bird to Nikita Gill (and of course those noted above). The characteristically informal and self-referential style of many Instapoets is at odds with the sorts of traditional critical literary expectations put forward by T. S. Eliot, which Celia Hunt and Fiona Sampson re-contextualise in *Writing: Self and Reflexivity.* "For T. S. Eliot, it was the poet's responsibility to contribute to the 'ideal order' of the 'existing monuments' of the literary tradition, by simultaneously working within that order and modifying it by the creation of new work". Such a perspective advocated—as Watts does in her article—that there should be "a continual surrender of himself as he is at the moment...to something which is more valuable" (Eliot cited in Hunt and Sampson 2005, 55). Eliot's preferred "state of impersonality" can be read as being diametrically opposed to the contemporary notion of literary celebrity in general and digital literary influencers specifically, given that, at times, the most prominent voices seem disinterested in the traditions from which the canon has been constructed.

Given this ideologically loaded context, it is perhaps not surprising that, on publication, Watts' article attracted largely hostile attention on social media. In her response to Watts' article, McNish rejected the suggestion that audience accessibility via digital platforms signified the demise of intellectual engagement and craft, saying "I also find it really patronising [...] when social media is constantly spoken about as if it is 'dumbing down' the world" (McNish 2018; italics in original). This syntactical slip (in referring to 'the world' rather than people) could equally be read as a narcissistic signifier (as Watts implies in her article) or a justifiable rebuff. After McNish posted a public response to Watts' article on her website, a Twitter-storm ensued, in which the majority of comments defended McNish and castigated Watts, stating in no uncertain terms that she was jealous and/or anti-feminist and/or elitist (both McNish and Watts studied at Cambridge University, and Watts is a published poet who has alluded to the lack of female writers in the canon). Comments on Twitter such as "[i]nsulting, deeply personal, elitism printed in prestigious journal" by bestselling author Kerry Hudson generated more than eighty likes, while poet Nick Garrard described the piece as "an ugly little blast of unreconstructed snobbery" (Hudson 2018; Garrard 2018).

Insta-Democracy

Many of the literary voices (such as Hudson and Garrard), who vociferously objected to Watts' article via Tweets, recognised the significance of social media in general, and Instapoets in particular, for the increase in interest in poetry among younger audiences and the potential for this market opportunity to affect engagement, not only in terms of culture but also in terms of some of the social, political and ideological issues of our time. The simplification of social issues via homespun verse can be seen to represent a more accessible entry point for readers online but also risks being ridiculed by the intellectual elite, who tend to denounce such musings as dumbing down (Fallon 2018; Ignatieff 2018). But this simplistic critical response to simplified storytelling online risks overlooking Instapoetry's contributing role in the growth of the poetry market.

In 2016, *Wired*, a California-based magazine that focuses on how emerging technologies affect culture, economics, and politics, published an article titled "Don't look now, but 2016 is resurrecting poetry" (Pandell 2016). Citing an exponential rise in engagement with poetry after the presidential election in the States in 2016, poems by writers such as Saladin Ahmed and Claudia Rankine, became the go-to online aphorisms for the collective fall out of the liberal left. According to Pandell, engagement with poets.org over two days, on and immediately after the election (8th and 9th November 2016, respectively), rose significantly, with more than 550 people tweeting poems (compared to typical two-day engagement statistics of 80–100 people tweeting links to its poets and 70–100 retweeting their posts) (Pandell 2016). More recently, Amanda Gorman, the first national youth poet laureate, gained over 2 million followers on Instagram in a day after delivering her poem at Joe Biden's inauguration (Chen 2021).

Like Kaur, Gorman is both a bestselling poet and a respected "brand", whose work is vaunted on business-facing platforms such as Forbes and Harvard Business Review (as well as being published on Instagram and via more traditional formats such as printed books). The correlation between her writing and her brand enables her to broaden the appeal of her work to the point at which she is able to influence the platforms upon which she performs and publishes her work (Bradt 2021). Both Kaur and Gorman have become feted style icons, which serves to reinforce their brand and influence. Kaur's Instafeed, for instance, is made up of curated poetic sketches and musings about identity and emotions, alongside aspirational professional photos of her. The dialogue between sketches such as "you can imitate a light like mine/but you cannot become it" (Kaur 2017) and visually arresting images of Kaur in traditional dress in front of the Taj Mahal proffers a brand strategy that communicates both access to the author's emotions and a distancing signified by the faux-regal style of fashion photography, epitomised in a photo shoot from *Cosmopolitan India*, who featured Kaur on their front page in 2018.

Because emotional vulnerability and social consciousness are inherent to their public personas, poets such as Amanda Gorman and Rupi Kaur are able to shine a spotlight on the canons and contexts in which they publish and perform and to call out injustice where they find it. This became apparent, for instance, in 2015, when Kaur posted a photograph of a woman on a bed with a period stain on her clothes and sheets. Instagram removed it from the site twice, which served to crystallise Kaur's position:

> Thank you Instagram for providing me with the exact response my work was created to critique. You deleted my photo twice stating that it goes against community guidelines. I will not apologize for not feeding the ego and pride of misogynist society that will have my body in underwear but not be okay with a small leak. When your pages are filled with countless photos/accounts where women (so many who are underage) are objectified, pornified and treated less than human. (Kaur 2015)

Instagram reinstated the photo (which, alongside the response above, has garnered 110,095 likes at the time of writing), evidencing a small but significant shift in power, as the author (Kaur) directly influenced the behaviour of her publishing platform (Instagram).[1]

BRANDING

Kaur's online activity has therefore disrupted the publishing praxis in two ways. Firstly, Kaur published online (on Instagram), then self-published and then, due to a growing demand, Andrews McMeel (notably a general publisher rather than a literary one) signed her up. Secondly, Kaur is so

---

[1] The significance of foregrounding the self in the pursuit of self-expression and self-efficacy forms an ongoing dialectic for female writers, which French feminist Hélène Cixous put forward in "The Laugh of the Medusa" in 1975. Cixous' epochal essay adjusts the mode of address towards the end of the article from direct, "And why don't you write?" (Cixous 1975, 876), to the third person, "She writes in white ink" (Cixous 1975, 881). The detachment inferred here, which suggests that a woman's relationship to their text and to the act of writing are fluid, is integral to the construction of a female public persona online, given the particular vitriol that women in the media spotlight tend to attract. Cixous' evocations of feminine difference as a catalyst for creativity and self-expression (jouissance even), rather than a cause for secrecy and shame, are significant for the current generation of Instapoets, who openly reject the constraints of both their sex and the literary canon.

influential that she is able to affect the behaviour of the platform she chooses to publish on (Instagram). Citing J. K. Rowling as a case in point (but equally relevant to Kaur), publisher Michael Bhaskar explains in *The Content Machine* that "When writers reach critical mass they transcend publishers" (Bhaskar 2013, 66). Rowling's website "disintermediated her publishers" because "her brand, the creative potential of digital technology and a devoted community" meant that she didn't need them for her expanded media franchise (Bhaskar 2013, 66).[2]

Kaur threatened to disintermediate her digital publishing platform, when she challenged Instagram with regard to the censorship of her period post, which took place in real time in front of an audience of millions. As an influencer, Kaur's cultural and economic capital allowed her to override the platform's editorial norms. Bhaskar notes that the emphasis has shifted from what Brian O'Leary describes as the "'container model' of publishing, whereby publishers fill 'containers', or books, with content, and then sell them. The suggestion is that the digital context, 'critical admixture' (such as hashtags) and metadata, fundamentally influence how a particular text performs in an online literary marketplace. (O'Leary cited in Bhaskar 2013, 15). Put simply, Kaur's hashtags could be said to have more influence on consumer behaviour than many traditional marketing campaigns within the publishing industry. In this way, writers such as Kaur are able to influence not only their followers but also, in small, incremental ways, the infrastructure of the publishing business.

Poets have historically been the least commercial writers in the canon, and yet Insta poets such as Rupi Kaur are now landing enviable publishing deals. This anomalous development has become the norm in a marketplace in which "The self today is an entrepreneurial self, a self that's packaged to be sold" (Deresiewicz 2011). Understood in this way, the self can be regarded as a malleable commodity to be repurposed on a variety of media sites, including videos such as YouTube, the personal websites of entrepreneurs, product-related sites and of course through writing (Smith and Watson 2017). As Yu points out in his Poetry Foundation article about the rise of the Instapoet and its place within the poetry world, "self-promotion and media manipulation" can be seen as central to the success of the most popular poets online (Yu 2019). Writers such as Kaur can be

---

[2] Jo Gill suggests in *Modern Confessional Writing: New Critical Essays* that the act of confession can be read as implying a degree of authenticity and authority in which subjectivity is foregrounded but that this perspective should be questioned (Gill 2006).

read as disrupting the mechanism for literary production and dissemination in sidelining publishers by speaking directly to—and perhaps more importantly discovering—their audiences. Kaur's audiences are disinterested in the establishment's preoccupation with the aesthetic value of her poetry and her brand. Her verse and sketches and her business as a poet-entrepreneur therefore form an unusual hybrid within the world of poetry. The market for poetry, after all, has historically been characterised by low advances and small print runs. Conversely, according to the *Atlantic*, Kaur approaches poetry like "running a business" (Hill and Yuan 2018).

The Entrepreneurial Self

Aarthi Vadde's article "Amateur creativity: Contemporary literature and the digital publishing scene", which discusses entrepreneurial behaviours within the digital literary space, is insightful here. In it, she suggests that the "'mass amateurization' of the critical, creative, and communicative arts, allow[s] amateurs to bypass the gatekeeping practices of specific institutions" (such as galleries, newspapers and publishing houses) (Vadde 2017, 27). Understood as those who produce and exchange content without being paid (rather than the more negative view of amateurism as denoting inferior quality), Vadde discusses how social media users within the literary domain have come up against the establishment as their projects gain attention and traction within the writing spaces set up for them to do precisely that. Vadde suggests that literary online influencers have the capacity to "build massive followings that operate entirely outside the professional literary circles that dictate prestige" (Vadde 2017, 38).

Part of the appeal of leading Instapoets is their status as "noble amateurs". They seem to be addressing their audiences directly and inviting them to respond accordingly. Smith and Watson suggest that "telling personal stories or performing one's sense of one's personality is critical to the conveyance of brand you" (Smith and Watson 2017). But branding the producer in this way can be seen as problematic in that it commodifies both the product and its creators. In "Clubs to Companies: Notes on the decline of political culture in speeded up creative worlds" cultural theorist Angela McRobbie explains that "Creative work increasingly follows the neo-liberal model, governed by the values of entrepreneurialism, individualization and reliance on commercial sponsorship" (McRobbie 2002). Since McRobbie's early insights on the commodification of the self in the twenty-first-century, digital micro-narratives—an appreciative emoji or a retweet—can be understood as contributing to the circulation of personal value. It follows that the "marketisation of everything" has become integral to mainstream cultural production (Mould 2018).

CONCLUSION

At a certain point of engagement, the content becomes less relevant than the context, as the discussion of Instapoets above shows. Watts' beleaguered viewpoint in *PN Review* was particularly significant because it drew attention to the marketisation of subjectivity through Instapoetry. In his article "How feelings took over the world" William Davies suggests that "If politics and public debate have become more emotional, as so many observers have claimed, this is as much a reflection of the speed and relentlessness of current media technologies as anything else" (Davies 2018). The frequency and velocity of digital communication are, Davies suggests, better suited to an emotional response than a considered rational one, and this is evident in the online debate following the publication of Watts' article.

In issue 146 of Granta (the magazine of new writing) titled *The Politics of Feeling*, the editors open with the question: "What should we do with our feelings? They've become so intemperate lately" (Baum and Appignanesi 2019, 10). This open-ended question seems apt as an ending to this chapter, since the issue is ongoing. Baum and Appignanesi go on to say that "Feelings summon those parts of ourselves that seem strange, dubious—foreign. As such, whenever we pronounce people too emotional to participate in politics, we should consider who historically has been labelled thus: ethnic minorities, for example, or women" (Baum and Appignanesi 2019, 10). Amanda Gorman and Rupi Kaur's poetry, for instance, may be troubling for the literary establishment not just because the work poses a threat to the value systems of a field which favours complexity but also because of their status as young women of colour expressing their emotions and generating significant economic and social capital in doing so (McQuillan 2018, 23).

REFERENCES

Baum, Devorah, and Josh Appignanesi. 2019. The Politics of Feeling. *Granta: The Magazine of New Writing* (Issue 146). London: Granta.

Beller, Thomas. 2013. The Ongoing Story: Twitter and Writing. *New Yorker*, June 18. https://www.newyorker.com/books/page-turner/the-ongoing-story-twitter-and-writing. Accessed 30 Aug 2019.

Bhaskar, Michael. 2013. *The Content Machine: Towards a Theory of Publishing from the Printing Press to the Digital Network*. London: Anthem.

Bradt, George. 2021. A Masterclass in Personal Branding by Amanda Gorman. *Forbes*, January 26. https://www.forbes.com/sites/georgebradt/2021/01/26/a--masterclass-in-personal-branding-from-amanda-gorman/?sh=f46e2093c8d9. Accessed 20 Feb 2021.

Chen, Tanya. 2021. Amanda Gorman Gained Over 2 Million IG Followers After Reading Her Poem at the Inauguration. *Buzzfeed*, January 22. https://www.buzzfeednews.com/article/tanyachen/amanda-gorman-gained-over-2-million-ig-followers. Accessed Feb 20.

Cixous, Hélène. 1975. The Laugh of the Medusa. In Keith Cohen and Paula Cohen. 1976. *Signs*: 1(4): 875–893. The University of Chicago Press.

Davies, William. 2018. *Nervous States: How Feeling Took Over the World*. London: Jonathan Cape.

Deresiewicz, William. 2011. Generation Sell. *The New York Times*, November 12. https://www.nytimes.com/2011/11/13/opinion/sunday/the-entrepreneurial-generation.html. Accessed 3 Sep 2019.

Eliot, T.S. 1982. Tradition and the Individual Talent. *Perspecta* 19: 36–42. The MIT Press on Behalf of Perspecta. http://www.jstor.org/stable/1567048.

Ezard, John. 2000. No Poetic Justice in Bestseller Lists. *The Guardian*, October 5. https://www.theguardian.com/uk/2000/oct/05/books.booksnews1. Accessed 3 Sept 2019.

Fallon, Claire. 2018. Instagram Poetry Is a Huckster's Paradise. *HuffPost*, October 4. https://www.huffingtonpost.co.uk/entry/instagram-poetry-atticus-duncan-penn_n_5bb2df2de4b0ba8bb2104b1b. Accessed 3 Sep 2019.

Garrard, Nick. Twitter Post. January 22, 2018. 12.36.p.m. https://twitter.com/havishambler/status/955418997922680833?s=21

Gill, Jo. 2006. *Modern Confessional Writing: New Critical Essays Psychology Press*. Abingdon-on-Thames: Psychology Press.

Hill, Faith and Karen Yuan. 2018. How Instagram Saved Poetry. *Atlantic*, October 15. https://www.theatlantic.com/technology/archive/2018/10/rupi-kaur-instagram-poet-entrepreneur/572746/. Accessed 1 Sept 2019.

Hudson, Kerry. Twitter Post. January 23, 2018. 1.58.p.m. https://twitter.com/thatkerryhudson/status/955801813223202816?s=21

Hunt, Celia, and Fiona Sampson. 2005. *Writing: Self and Reflexivity*. London: Palgrave.

Ignatieff, Michael. 2018. Is Identity Politics Ruining Democracy? *Financial Times*, September 5. https://www.ft.com/content/09c2c1e4-ad05-11e8-8253-48106866cd8a. Accessed 30 Aug 2019.

Kaur, Rupi. 2015. Thank You Instagram. Instagram, March 24. https://www.instagram.com/p/0ovWwJHA6f/?hl=en. Accessed 30 Aug 2019.

————. 2017. To Heal… Instagram, December 19. https://www.instagram.com/p/Bc3cc-2g86t/?hl=en. Accessed 30 June 2020.

Larson, Jeremy D. 2019. Why Do We Obsess Over What's 'Relatable'? *New York Times Magazine*, 8 January. https://www.nytimes.com/2019/01/08/magazine/the-scourge-of-relatable-in-art-and-politics.html. Accessed 30 Aug 2019.

McNish, Holly. 2018. *PN Review*. Author Website, January 21. https://holliepoetry.com/2018/01/21/pn-review/. Accessed 1 Sept 2019.

McQuillan, David. 2018. *Aesthetic Scandal and Accessibility: The Subversive Simplicity of Rupi Kaur's Milk and Honey*. PhD Dissertation, University of Halifax.

McRobbie, Angela. 2002. Clubs to Companies: Notes on the Decline of Political Culture in Speeded Up Creative Worlds. *Cultural Studies* 16 (4): 516–531. https://doi.org/10.1080/09502380210139098.

Mould, Oli. 2018. *Against Creativity*. London: Verso.

Murray, Simone. 2012. *The Adaptation Industry: The Cultural Economy of Contemporary Literary Adaptation*. Abingdon: Routledge.

Oates, Joyce Carol. Twitter Post. November 30 2012. 7.46 p.m. https://twitter.com/JoyceCarolOates/status/274600367445139456

O'Neil, Luke. 2019. Delete Your Account: Leaving Facebook Can Make You Happier, Study Finds. *The Guardian*, February 1. https://www.theguardian.com/technology/2019/feb/01/facebook-mental-health-study-happiness-delete-account. Accessed 30 Aug 2019.

Pandell, Lexi. 2016. Don't Look Now, But 2016 Is Resurrecting Poetry. *Wired*, November 22. https://www.wired.com/2016/11/poetry-popularity-on-twitter/. Accessed 30 Aug 2019.

Smith, Sidonie, and Julia Watson. 2017. *Life Writing in the Long Run: A Smith & Watson Autobiography Studies Reader*. Ann Arbor: Michigan Publishing/University of Michigan Library. https://doi.org/10.3998/mpub.9739969.

Soat, Molly. 2015. Social Media Triggers a Dopamine High. November 13. https://docs.google.com/document/d/1XB2O6Krq8_7hEsa_KW5gNVJimNn5EmMUXhlG-kAaft0/edit#. Accessed 15 July 2020.

Squires, Claire. 2007. *Marketing Literature: The Making of Contemporary Writing in Britain*. London: Palgrave.

Underwood, Jack. 2019. This quote is from an online survey I ran between January and March 2019. (See Appendix).

Vadde, Aarthi. 2017. Amateur Creativity: Contemporary Literature and the Digital Publishing Scene. *New Literary History* 48 (1 Winter): 27–51, 194.

Watts, Rebecca. 2018. The Cult of the Noble Amateur. *PN Review 239* 44: 3. https://www.pnreview.co.uk/cgi-bin/scribe?item_id=10090. Accessed 25 July 2019.

Wood, Heloise. 2018. Watts Slams "Amateur" Poetry of Kaur, McNish and Tempest. *Bookseller*, January 23. https://www.thebookseller.com/news/watts-questions-poetry-kaur-mcnish-and-tempest-712346. Accessed 25 July 2019.

Yu, Timothy. 2019. Instagram Poetry and Our Poetry Worlds. Poetry Foundation, April 24. https://www.poetryfoundation.org/harriet/2019/04/instagram-poetry-and-our-poetry-worlds. Accessed 3 Sept 2019.

CHAPTER 6

From Fidelity Publishing to Playable Stories

Nobody really knows where technology is heading and space is limitless, so it follows that publishers and developers have adopted the business model of throwing everything at the wall and then seeing what will stick. As a journalist, I found it variously silly and exciting and it certainly forced me out of my comfort zone, which is entirely healthy. As a consumer, though, I tend to read journalism online and literature in books. A paperback is still the best, most user-friendly piece of technology. (Xan Brooks, author of *The Clocks in This House All Tell Different Times*, 2019)

The concept of digital in the context of publishing has yet to be played out in ways that fully divert and convert publishers, scholars and readers (Horne 2017). Social psychologist Robert Zajonc's long-standing work on the pleasure of the familiar offers insights for better understanding the uneasy avoidance that humans (and other animals) exhibit when exposed to something new or unknown and can be applied to Brooks' apparent reluctance to experiment with digital formats, despite the widespread success of Kindles as alternatives to the printed text (Zajonc 1980). The conundrum for the book industry hinges on persuading consumers that digital is better than print while lacking that conviction themselves. Industry insider Molly Flatt similarly suggested in The *Bookseller* that publishing is the industry that "gets there in the end but [is] painfully slow" (Flatt 2018). Arnaud Nourry, chief executive of Hachette Livre (one of the "big five" publishing concerns), concludes that "We've tried enhanced or enriched ebooks—didn't work. We've tried apps, websites with our content—we have one or two successes among a hundred failures. I'm talking about the entire industry. We've not done very well" (Nourry cited in Flood 2018). It could be argued that traditional trade publishing's "pleasure in the familiar" is connected to its perceived identity within the creative industries as a late adopter. This chapter will therefore explore how the "pleasure of the familiar" presents challenges for publishing, in terms of form, content and audiences.

ADAPTATION

The resulting awareness of the impact of digital content on our lives is part of the reason why the term "digital age" already seems a bit old fashioned. Naming our digital-first culture in this way could be read as implying that digital is an economic and social characteristic of our age, rather than an embedded mode of communication and identification (Turkle 2011; Lanier 2018). Examining the psychological pull of the past can help us to better understand why collective cultural resistance to change informs individual consumer behaviour. From Zajonc's perspective, humans often resist change because of the uncertainty they feel "when exposed to a novel stimulus", but, through repeated exposure, the fear usually subsides (Montoya et al. 2017, 459). The idea of resisting change is a recurring theme in *The Adaptation Industry: The Cultural Economy of Contemporary Literary Adaptation,* in which Simone Murray explores the relationship between film and literature and suggests that literature has historically been idealised within adaptation studies by "fidelity criticism"—that insular division of theorists who view filmic adaptations of literary texts on the whole as a "betrayal" and "corruption" of the original work (Murray 2012). Fidelity criticism has a particular relevance for the literary, a heritage industry whose canonical trajectory and cultural capital are rooted in the past.

Fidelity studies foregrounds the original literary text in the context of subsequent convergent reworkings of the concept and narrative, most often through screen-based or multimedia adaptations. It questions the notion that "Repetition without replication bring[s] together the comfort of ritual and recognition with the delight of surprise and novelty" (Cartnell 2012, 31). Innovations such as Short Édition chime with fidelity studies' understanding of how the notion of the original text, and the perception of innate literary value, appeals to some readers. Short Édition, a free story dispenser installed in London (among other cities), issues eco-friendly papyrus paper stories to "Loiterers and Literati Alike". The vending machines have been compared to Penguin publishing founder Allen Lane's "Penguincubator", which was used to sell cheap paperbacks in the 1930s (Flood 2019). Fidelity publishing studies, understood here as a subset of fidelity criticism, foregrounds the history of publishing and emphasises a perceived tension in the relationship between print and digital which is inherently nostalgic (Van der Weel et al. 2018), a polarised perspective that risks becoming obsolete in this networked age. Remediation is important because it can be used as a mechanism for testing not only the efficacy of material production (e.g. updating and upgrading devices) but also the conformity of the systems of material production themselves.

In *The Gutenberg Galaxy* McLuhan's "rear view mirror" theory is applied to the recurring dynamic between technological advances and consumer resistance. Johannes Gutenberg is widely regarded as having invented the printing press in the fifteenth century and the advent of the printing press was a moment of great cultural significance, since it meant that knowledge could be mass reproduced by a machine (rather than laboriously copied by hand). In keeping with Zajonc's theory of the familiar, McLuhan's "rear view mirror" idea suggests that we "attach ourselves to the objects, to the flavor of the most recent past" which signifies an ambivalence to technological change that is coloured by nostalgia and characterised by foot-dragging (Meikle 2009, 87; McLuhan and Fiore 1967, 74–75). Shaking off such entrenched mindsets is challenging, which may be why experiments with form in publishing often amount to little more than a palimpsest of digital functionality being overlaid onto a pre-existing text. Research by digital bookseller Kobo, for instance, shows that growing demographics of eBook readers, such as women in mid-life onwards, benefit from the convenience provided by the format, which is enjoyed in part because it emulates a traditional book (the structure of which has changed little since the invention of Gutenberg's printing press) (Flood 2016). The eBook's reputation for technological conservatism (a close relative of fidelity criticism) is a case in point (Rowberry 2017). This may also be why the "choose your own adventure" approach to adaptations (which is discussed later in this chapter in the context of Charlie Brooker's Netflix programme *Bandersnatch*) is frequently applied to the gamification of literary narratives, since it is a tried and tested format.

The discussion that follows focuses on case studies that have captured the attention of audiences by playing with preconceived ideas of experience and engagement at the intersection of literature and technology. These encounters tend to occur within a convergent digital space. In *Convergence Culture: Where Old and New Media Collide*, Henry Jenkins defines convergence culture as "the flow of content across multiple media platforms, the cooperation between multiple media industries, and the migratory behavior of media audiences" (Jenkins 2006, 2–4). Convergence culture is sometimes misunderstood as simply enacting a process of remediation, in which seemingly outdated narrative forms are superseded by more "culturally relevant" ones. But Jenkins points out that convergence is less to do with technology than mindset: "Convergence does not occur through media appliances, however sophisticated they may become. Convergence occurs within the brains of individual consumers and through their social interactions with others" (Jenkins 2006, 3). The next section considers the dynamic between convergent culture, literary media and the attention economy.

CONVERGENT CULTURE

Writing and publishing are experienced (or ignored) within an attention economy, by which I mean that the attention span of readers is a commodity that is subject to market forces. Yves Citton goes further, describing the way we move between types of content, from advertising to literature online, as an attention ecology (Glavey 2017). Put simply, the more time that audiences spend on particular websites, for instance, the more likely they are to buy—or buy into—associated products and ideas. According to Joseph Pine and James Gilmore, the experience economy feeds the attention economy because the quality of our digital experience affects engagement and "dwell time" (Pine and Gilmore [1999] 2019). Because immersive experiences, such as a live literature event or a Virtual Reality game, encourage greater dwell time, they represent a shift from product to experience, which opens up opportunities for participatory culture, which Jenkins sees as an ideologically beneficial outcome of convergence. As Hannah Wood notes, the market for playable stories, which is inherently more disruptive than traditional trade publishing, is opening up, with "Practitioners, publishers, investors, producers, academics and audiences...collaborating and competing to understand exactly how this form of storytelling works" (Wood 2016, 19). The growth of playable, participatory digital narratives (or convergence culture) is "getting defined top-down by decisions being made in corporate boardrooms and bottom-up by decisions made in teenagers' bedrooms" (Jenkins 2006). The benefits for audiences are evident in the value that stems from the "intensity of the consumer experience" rather than the "intrinsic value of the product itself" (Pine and Gilmore [1999] 2019, 3–4). The attention and the experience economy can therefore be viewed as two parts of the same "sell", if attention is understood as a commodity that can be traded in return for, at best, intense (and therefore memorable) experiences (and, at worst, clickbait and pop-up ads).[1]

The discourses and debates around digital publishing, and publishing that utilises digital technology, represent a broader shift in terms of consumer expectations, as Pine and Gilmore suggest, namely, the economic and social value of products in relation to experiences. Product-based digital publishing has (thus far) been more commercially viable for publishers and is concerned with the growth of non-print formats, which often emulate the narrative delivery and/or follow the publication of the printed text. Experience-based publishing focuses more on experiments with form, in terms of digital narrative projects ranging from gaming and virtual reality to digital-first novels, that is, eBooks that pilot novel formats and follies within the literary sphere. The next part of this chapter will explore experiments with form that play out these positions, with particular reference to Faber's *Waste Land* app, Stephen King's Kindle novella *Ur*, Iain Pears novel *Arcadia*, Duncan Speakman's ambient book *It Must Have Been Dark by Then* and Charlie Brooker's Netflix episode *Bandersnatch*.

THE WASTE LAND

The release of Faber's digital edition of *The Waste Land* in 2011 was the result of a collaborative venture with Touch Press, an app development agency. Viewed at the time as being a game changer, in terms of the potential for publishing to expand both the narrative experience and its audiences, the app contained a number of enhancement features. These included a specially filmed performance of the poem by actress Fiona Shaw, audio readings of the poem by T. S. Eliot and actor and publisher

---

[1] *The Experience Economy* charts the progression of economic value in a trajectory from goods through to services then on to experiences (Pine and Gilmore 1999).

Viggo Mortensen (among other luminaries), as well as comprehensive interactive notes and digitised original manuscript pages, so that the viewer could see how the poem took shape under Ezra Pound's editorial guidance.

This additional material can be read as an ambitious attempt by the publisher to position the narrative as a convergent text and expanded reading experience. But, in my view, the central position of the original poem remains unassailable since the metanarratives are less remediation than adulation. In other words, Faber repurposed the content faithfully (rather than disruptively), although the app was viewed as being ground-breaking at the time. The verse remains central, the app *adds to* Eliot's work, through various mediums, voices and perspectives. The ability to, for instance, flip between readers' voices via a single tap, so that a particular passage alters in tone and delivery, could be read as mirroring the fractured authority of Eliot's text with its multiple assembled voices. However, like the poem itself, the "visionary alternative" that the app grapples with is bound by its treatment of the poem, in that all interpretations and interventions—filmic, audio and editorial—form iterative responses to the original text (rather than self-generating ones). This meant that the app was important as an advanced tool for mapping out and connecting interpretations by cultural intermediaries (from actors to coders) which promoted remediated experiences with the text. Thus the legacy of the project lay partly in its implicit acknowledgement that staging enhanced reading experiences was necessary, in terms of using digital technology to diversify revenue streams.

UR AND ARCADIA

Staging experiential encounters with literary media in order to promote sales also informed the online launch of Stephen King's free novella, *Ur*, which was published exclusively for Amazon's Kindle in 2009 (Flood 2009). King was one of the first mainstream American writers to whole-heartedly embrace the digital possibilities for sharing his stories, following on from the successful adaptation of so many of his horror novels into films. Amazon used its platform as a stage to engage customers in a way that would create a memorable event. King's novella—an unsettling story about an e-reader that can access books and newspapers from alternate worlds—coalesced with the experiential promise of the platform itself, which generated an early surge of interest in Kindles. As a brand building exercise, the publication of *Ur* benefitted the author, platform and publisher at a time before Amazon's reputation was subject to the level of scrutiny it is today. It also, in a sense, invited the reader to actively partici- pate in the process of remediation, in which the success or failure of King's experiment would signify the reader's response to the format.

In the UK, Iain Pears' world-hopping novel *Arcadia* was released as an interactive, self-directed app two weeks before it was published as a hard- back book (Amphio Limited 2018). The strategy of publishing digital-first for free, or for as little as 99p, has become an accepted promotional prac- tice among publishers keen to secure early reviews and elevate rankings. Once audience engagement begins to grow, publishers can expedite the release of the full-price print edition and so begin to generate more signifi- cant sales (Cocozza 2017).[2] That publishers were, in a sense, gaming the system through their digital publishing strategy was not lost on Pears, who, in an article in *The Guardian* in 2015 (which promoted both the app and the book), noted the limitations of the form: "eBooks are now quite venerable in computing terms, but it is striking how small an impact they have had on narrative structure; for the most part, they are still just ordi- nary books in a cheap format" (Pears 2015). The primary role of eBooks could therefore be read as promulgating cheap content and promotional opportunities rather than promoting experimental writing.

Pears' statement above recognises the limitations of eBooks, in terms of experiments with form which more specialised and performative types of digital writing such as E-lit attempt to subvert. In terms of audience and genre conventions, E-lit is distinct from stories packaged in mainstream digital content "containers" such as eBooks and podcasts and expresses form *as* content in which born-digital texts, such as hypertexts, constitute the story (Hayle 2007). The digital format for eBooks, on the other hand, is primarily a means to an end (both figuratively and financially), since it functions as a conduit for the story. Games designer Hannah Wood cites Marie-Laure Ryan's explanation of the ecology of digital writing in "From Narrative Games to Playable Stories: Toward a Poetics of Interactive Narrative", which illuminates this "split condition":

---

[2] Generating interest in products, and engaging communities in dialogue around those products, promotes what psychologist Robert Cialdini in *Influence: The Psychology of Persuasion* (2009) describes as reciprocal behaviour; namely, that if you are given something for free, you're more likely to have positive associations with the relevant individual, brand or organisation, and may therefore be more likely to spend money with them in future.

[The] categorisation of the "split condition" of digital narrative into The North Pole (the home of experimental literature), the Tropics (the home of popular culture), and the Temperate Zone between (the home of 'serious' literary authors), is a useful theoretical framework for understanding the differences between genres. (Ryan 2007; Wood 2016, 8)

THE SPLIT CONDITION

In the context of Ryan's territories above, a novel such as *Arcadia* would be located within the Temperate Zone—"the home of 'serious' literary authors". But as an app that was developed and launched briefly in advance of the novel, *Arcadia* was an experiment with form in which each line was designed to "represent the journey of a different character [as] they twist and intersect at nodes before branching out once more, until all finally meet again at the ending" (Poole 2015). What Pears' digitised fiction reveals is a discomfort with the limitations and expectations of the split condition. Although readers select routes through the novel, ultimately they end up at the same conclusion. Moving beyond the constraints of a narrative form that is itself emulating the immersive possibilities of gaming is structurally challenging, as Fron, Fullerton, Morie and Pearce explain:

Video games, on the whole, tend to be organized around game structures…which demands logical structure and therefore lends itself to strict rule sets; it may also be due to the prevalence of male designers in the field who may tend to favor more ludic, goal-oriented forms of play. (Fron et al. 2007, 3)

"BANDERSNATCH"

Like *Arcadia*, "Bandersnatch" is a branching-path narrative (in film form), which is organised around game structures and situates the viewer as spectator-director, thus creating a narrative game experience (Jost 2020). The "Bandersnatch" episode was part of Charlie Brooker's dystopian *Black Mirror* series on Netflix and appears to favour a "goal-oriented" approach to play, despite the diversions en route (Fron et al. 2007, 3). "Bandersnatch" was inspired by, and openly references, the choose your own adventure series of gamebooks which peaked in popularity in the 1980s and which allowed the reader to assume the role of protagonist and to make choices which would determine the outcome (Lavin 2020).

"Bandersnatch" can be viewed passively as a television programme, or actively, if the viewer chooses to use their remote to respond to the choices presented to them. The narrative pathways, which the viewer can intermittently determine, range from mundane and seemingly meaningless decisions such as which cereal protagonist Stefan should eat for breakfast, to whether to "fight your therapist" or jump out of the window (Jost 2020, 168–9). Stefan's feeling of being constantly controlled forms part of the narrative tension, since the viewer/player is invited to dial this tension up or down through the choices they make and the resultant version that they watch. In this way, the viewer becomes implicated in the story as it unfolds.

"Bandersnatch" demonstrates that playable narratives can be viewed as both a form of remediation, "in which one medium is seen by our culture as reforming or improving upon another" (Bolter and Grusin 2000, 59; Jost 2020), and a performative encounter. This shift in how the user or viewer is perceived opens up possibilities in terms of what immersive technology can offer readers. Wood discusses a similar issue in the context of gaming, particularly in relation to Ryan's narrative dichotomy:

> The combination of narrativity and interactivity oscillates between two forms: the narrative game, in which narrative meaning is subordinated to the player's actions, and the playable story, in which the player's actions are subordinated to narrative meaning. Or, to put it differently, in a narrative game, story is meant to enhance gameplay, while in a playable story, gameplay is meant to produce story. (Wood 2016, 22; Ryan 2009, 45)

Playable stories encourage participants to co-create narratives, rather than performing pre-determined characters and outcomes. Participation is therefore seen as adding value to the experience of viewing, in that, through taking part or assuming a performative role within the narrative, the experience becomes more memorable. In his discussion of "Bandersnatch", Jost concludes that a shift has occurred in relation to the remediated role of the audience, in terms of "watching" television:

> What do I call what has been a user until now? A word combined with "actor" would be possible, provided it were specified that it is more in the sense of an actor who plays a text written by someone else than as an acting actor. Faced with the cumbersomeness it generates, I prefer to dismiss it. Operator, performer, player...and if this user were simply called an "interpreter?" (Jost 2020, 172)

Experiential Stories

Jost's rhetorical questions allude to the changing dynamic between the audience and the text in an era of playable stories. Ambient literature, an emergent field of literary media that is produced through dynamic encounters between technology, location and readers, is similarly invested in immersive experiences. Using data from smartphones in order to personalise the act of reading, ambient stories often respond to external factors such as weather and time as devices that generate idiosyncratic narrative encounters linked to emotional states. Intensifying experiential encounters is a characteristic of the genre, as is evident in *Breathe* by Kate Pullinger, one of the proponents of ambient literature's approach. *Breathe* is an ambient ghost story published by Editions At Play with Visual Editions, which is described as a personalised book on Visual Editions' website (Pullinger 2018). The narrator begins by asking for the reader/listener's location, after which local place names are integrated into the story. This approach is similarly integrated into an early section of Duncan Speakman's *It Must Have Been Dark by Then* (there are no page numbers), in which Speakman situates the reader in a liminal space:

> I'm looking at a Google map on the screen of my phone. Even though I know these are projections, not copies of the world, I am already trying to picture what the places might be like. My imagination is rooted in fictional depictions of the unforgiving desert and mysterious swamp dwellers. (Speakman 2017)

By foregrounding immersive narrative experiences that link digital and analogue text in new ways and which draw on locative information to enact a spoken word story, Speakman invites readers/participants to renegotiate urban cartography. The place referred to in the text (which was partly user-generated) generates a peculiarly disorientating process that is neither singularly immersive (like an online game) nor wholly distracting (like a book).

Ambient literature represents a significant development, in terms of its potential to link to atmospheric stimuli by connecting with home automation systems, for instance. But, so far, most ambient lit is restricted to limited personalisation based on location. User-generated experiences and communities tend to gain traction when grounded within measurable, physical performative spaces as is evident in apps such as Nike's Me-to-We

Nike Plus membership project. In *Principles of Participation* by Nina Simon, the author compares digital innovations within museum and gallery spaces to the Nike Plus community project, suggesting that much can be learnt from the leading sports brand: "Nike+ took an uncontrolled venue—the streets and trails used by runners all over the world—and created a compelling experience around it. For its users, Nike+ transforms running into a pervasive, fun, socially driven experience" (Simon 2010).

Narrative encounters offered through ambient literature are often limited to a singular experience, while Nike+ is concerned with brand building through community building, which is increasingly relevant in this digitally distanced age. Perhaps this is why the performative aspect of theatre, live literature and sport continue to hold a particular appeal to audiences. As Josephine Machon explains in *Immersive Theatres: Intimacy and Immediacy in Contemporary Performance*: "The alienation from real intimacy in our workaday lives, via such forums as Facebook, can be addressed by immersive practice, which demands bodily engagement, sensually stimulates the imagination, requires tactility" (Machon 2013, 26). The appeal of "installation and intimacy", for instance, in the interdisciplinary work of artists such as Yoko Ono and Marina Abramovich, and in the immersive theatrical productions of companies such as Punch Drunk and Mercurial Wrestler, attract audiences seeking to temporarily disengage from the state of distractedness that is a characteristic of this digital age (Machon 2013, 33).

Conclusion

This chapter set out to examine how the "pleasure of the familiar" presents challenges for publishing, in terms of form, digital content and audiences. It has discussed case studies that represent a sliding scale of experimentation at the intersection of literature, storytelling and technology and has considered the role of performance, environment and play as recurring elements within the personalised digital narrative encounters discussed above. While hyper-personalised "frictionless" consumer experiences are standard for brands such as Nike, such developments have yet to be fully integrated into the creative industries generally and the literary industries specifically. Personalising the way in which audiences interact with stories online is a necessary aspect of innovation and will be integral to the diversification of representation, narrative possibilities and audiences online.

REFERENCES

Brooks, Xan. 2019. This quote is from an online survey I ran between January and March 2019 (See Appendix).

Cartnell, Deborah. 2012. Familiarity Versus Contempt: Becoming Jane and the Adaptation Genre. In *Adaptation and Cultural Appropriation: Literature, Film and the Arts*, ed. Nicklas Pascal and Oliver Lindner. Berlin: De Gruyter.

Cocozza, Paula. 2017. The How eBooks Lost Their Shine: "Kindles Now Look Clunky and Unhip". *The Guardian*, April 27. https://www.theguardian.com/books/2017/apr/27/how-ebooks-lost-their-shine-kindles-look-clunky-unhip-. Accessed 13 May 2018.

Flatt, Molly. 2018. "I Can't Think of Another Industry that Makes Decisions in Such a Void": Rachel Botsman on Books and Trust. *Bookseller*, October 24.

Flood, Alison. 2009. Stephen King Writes Ebook Horror Story for New Kindle. *The Guardian*, February 10. https://www.theguardian.com/books/2009/feb/10/stephen-king-kindle-ur. Accessed 10 June 2018.

———. 2016. Digital Reading Driven by Older Women. *The Guardian*, April 15. https://www.theguardian.com/books/2016/apr/15/digital-reading-driven-by-older-women-study-claims. Accessed 11 May 2018.

———. 2018. "Ebooks Are Stupid", Says Head of One of World's Biggest Publishers. *The Guardian*, 20 February. https://www.theguardian.com/books/2018/feb/20/ebooks-are-stupid-hachette-livre-arnaud-nourry Accessed 11 May 2018.

———. 2019. Short Story Vending Machines to Transport London Commuters. *The Guardian*, April 2. https://www.theguardian.com/books/2019/apr/02/short-story-vending-machines-london-commuters-canary-wharf-anthony-horowitz. Accessed 1 July 2019.

Fron, Janine, Tracy Fullerton, Jacquelyn Ford Morie, and Celia Pearce. 2007. Playing Dress-Up: Costumes, Roleplay and Imagination. In *Philosophy of Computer Games*, 24–27. http://www.ludica.org.uk/LudicaDress-Up.pdf. Accessed 10 June 2018.

Glavey, Brian. 2017. Poetry and the Attention Economy. *Contemporary Literature* 58 (3): 423–429.

Hayle, Katherine. 2007. Electronic Literature: What Is It? The Electronic Literature Organization, January 2. https://eliterature.org/pad/elp.html. Accessed 14 Feb 2021.

Horne, Alastair. 2017. Publishing: The Last (and Next?) Five Years. *The Indexer: The International Journal of Indexing* 35: 2–9.

Jenkins, Henry. 2006. *Convergence Culture: Where Old and New Media Collide*. New York: New York University Press.

Jost, François. 2020. What Kind of Art is the Cinema of Interactions? In *Post-cinema, Cinema in the Post-art Era*, ed. Dominique Chateau and Jose Moure. Amsterdam University Press.

Lanier, Jaron. 2018. *Ten Arguments for Deleting Your Social Media Accounts Right Now*. London: Random House.

Lavin, Will. 2020. Netflix Is Being Sued by Children's Book Publisher Over "Black Mirror: Bandersnatch". *NME*, February 15. https://www.nme.com/news/tv/netflix-black-mirror-bandersnatch-sued-childrens-book-publisher-2609867. Accessed 10 Jan 2021.

Machon, Josephine. 2013. *Immersive Theatres: Intimacy and Immediacy in Contemporary Performance*. Basingstoke: Macmillan.

McLuhan, Marshall, and Quentin Fiore. 1967. *The Medium is the Massage: An Inventory of Effects*. London: Random House.

Meikle, Graham. 2009. *Interpreting News*. London: Palgrave Macmillan.

Montoya, R.M., R.S. Horton, J.L. Vevea, M. Citkowicz, and E.A. Lauber. 2017. A Re-examination of the Mere Exposure Effect: The Influence of Repeated Exposure on Recognition, Familiarity, and Liking. *Psychological Bulletin* 143 (5): 459–498. https://doi.org/10.1037/bul0000085A.

Murray, Simone. 2012. *The Adaptation Industry: The Cultural Economy of Contemporary Literary Adaptation*. Abingdon: Routledge.

Pears, Iain. 2015. *Arcadia*. London: Vintage.

Pine, B. Joseph, and James, H. Gilmore. 1999. *The Experience Economy: Work Is Theatre & Every Business a Stage*. Boston: Harvard Business Press.

Poole, Steve. 2015. *Arcadia* by Iain Pears Review – A Fantastical Extravaganza. *The Guardian*, September 11. https://www.theguardian.com/books/2015/sep/11/arcadia-iain-pears-review. Accessed 10 June 2018.

Pullinger, Kate. 2018. *Breathe*. Visual Editions. https://editionsatplay.withgoogle.com/#!/detail/free-breathe. Accessed 16 July 2020.

Rowberry, Simon. 2017. Is the E-book a Dead Format? *Bookseller*, July 24. https://www.thebookseller.com/futurebook/ebook-dead-format-595431. Accessed 14 July 2020.

Ryan, Marie-Laure. 2007. Beyond Ludus: Narrative, Video Games and the Split Condition of Digital Textuality. In *Videogame, Player, Text*, ed. Tanya Krzywinska and Barry Atkins, 8–28. Manchester: Manchester University Press.

———. 2009. From Narrative Games to Playable Stories: Toward a Poetics of Interactive Narrative. *Storyworlds: A Journal of Narrative Studies* 1: 43–59. https://doi.org/10.1353/stw.0.0003.

Simon, Nina. 2010. *The Participatory Museum*. http://www.participatorymuseum.org/read/. Accessed 20 Jan 2021.

Speakman, Duncan. 2017. *It Must Have Been Dark by Then*. Bristol: Ambientlit.

Turkle, Sherry. 2011. *Alone Together: Why We Expect More from Technology and Less from Each Other*. New York: Basic Books.

Van der Weel, A, A. Phillips, R. Wischenbart, and M. Kovač. 2018. What Is a Book? Plenary at the By the Book Conference, Florence.

Wood, Hannah. 2016. *Playable Stories: Writing and Design Methods for Negotiating Narrative and Player Agency*. Exeter: University of Exeter. https://ore.exeter.ac.uk/repository/handle/10871/29281

Zajonc, Robert Boleslaw. 1980. Feeling and Thinking: Preferences Need No Inferences. *American Psychologist* 35: 117–123. https://doi.org/10.1037/0003-066X.35.2.151.

CHAPTER 7

Marketing True Lies and Autofiction

Being published has always been about 'creating the name of the author' although it's more complex than ever in a digital age. It's going to happen, it's part of the publishing process. Even anonymous authors, by choosing not to share their 'real' identity, are creating a persona. So I feel I may as well embrace it and contribute to the creation of the author brand, on a book by book basis. (Liz Flanagan 2019)

As novelist Liz Flanagan's statement above suggests, contemporary authors are frequently encouraged by their publishers to build their brand through their content strategy and social media presence in order to promote engagement and sales.[1] As discussed in Chap. 4, the author brand can take on its own narrative journey in which the brand is, in a sense, a further text (Underwood 2019). Understandably, some writers prefer to withdraw from this process; to step away from the glare of the digital limelight in order to evade the volatility of online criticism, compulsive "like" scoring and the threat of digital vigilantes (AKA online trolls). Elena Ferrante (pen name of the writer behind the bestselling four-part series of Neapolitan novels), for instance, has attracted international media attention in part because of the mystery she exudes in keeping her real identity secret. Ferrante declined to speak to the press until 2015, when she was interviewed for *The Paris Review* by her Italian publishers. During the

---

[1] The publishers of this book, for instance, ask for social media statistics in the proposal.

© The Author(s), under exclusive license to Springer Nature Switzerland AG 2021
A. Kiernan, *Writing Cultures and Literary Media*, New Directions in Book History, https://doi.org/10.1007/978-3-030-75081-7_7

exchange, she referred to "domesticating the truth" as a form of cliché, as "betraying the story out of laziness, out of acquiescence, out of convenience, out of fear" (Ferri 2015). For Ferrante, then, exposure risks inhibiting the act of storytelling.

The discomfort surrounding self-promotion and exposure online is something that books journalist and memoirist Cathy Rentzenbrink similarly recognises as being problematic for writers. She elaborated on her own complex relationship with social media in 2019, explaining that "I don't do any social media anymore because I don't like the way it makes me feel". Rentzenbrink went on to explain that:

> I used to narrate my life a lot on Twitter and Facebook but became uncomfortable with that almost at the same time as I started publishing memoirs. Feeling overexposed, perhaps? Or the oddness of posting throwaway comments about stacking the dishwasher while working on a long form narrative about grief that wouldn't be out for over a year. (Rentzenbrink 2019)

Rentzenbrink's reference to alternating between life-changing events and mundane trivia (domesticity) reveals the disjunct at the heart of digital self-promotion. Audiences often admire celebrities or a favourite author for being "other" than them, in the sense that they can be imagined as existing within a state of hyperreal success, influence and/or wealth, in terms of their status, and achievements. The unwritten rule of social media is that sharing a snapshot of domesticity is acceptable but divulging what lies beneath the sanitised surface (if that happens to be angst or anger) may alienate followers. But posts that share "true lies" or partial truths are problematic, particularly in the context of literature, a mode of expression characterised by its ability to ask difficult questions in order to create relevant work.

The success or failure of each of the marketing stories in this chapter centres on the authors' proximity to (or distance from) the demands of digital culture. Williams and Knausgård's slow novels offer a counterpoint to digital velocity, Ferrante fascinates by rejecting the demands of a publishing industry preoccupied by personalities, and the appeal of writers such as Boyle and Lockwood lies partly in their ability to express their anxiety and compulsion in response to digital culture. It is therefore interested in the relationship between fiction, non-fiction and online communication as flawed indicators of "authenticity" in an era characterised by the demise of cultural gatekeepers online.

TRUE LIES AND THE NEW JOURNALISM

Publishing "true lies" is part of a rich literary tradition which has its roots in journalism. In 1719, Daniel Defoe published *Robinson Crusoe* as a work of non-fiction, though it was later revealed to be fiction (Mullan 2018). This eighteenth-century marketing manoeuvre was based on the supposition that a memoir would be received more favourably by critics and audiences than a novel (a form deemed disreputable at the time).

One of the guiding principles of journalism is that the facts—the who, what, when, where, why (the five "ws")—should tell the story (Singer 2008). But without colour, reporting based on the five "ws" risks falling flat (and not being read), so journalists are encouraged to seek human interest stories in order to create engaging narratives. In "What journalism can offer ethnography", Walt Harrington describes journalists as "the junkyard dogs of ethnography" in that they unearth stories and furnish them with hooks to reel their readers in (Harrington 2003). Nowadays, journalists' click-targets feed the public's appetite for exposés via headlines online that bait the audience through tales of intrigue and emotion. This is something that the New Journalists' immersive countercultural forays in the 1960s inadvertently paved the way for, rejecting as they did the objective news writing norms of the time. Hunter S. Thompson famously lived among the subjects of his scoops, partly in order to ensure that his stories were based on lived experiences and observations. Of course, this high-risk story-seeking strategy wasn't without retributive recourse. (Thompson was badly beaten up by the Hell's Angels he wrote about, for instance.)

Memoir writing delivers against different expectations than journalism, despite both forms finding meaning as arbiters of "truth". Reportage is accountable against a code of conduct which espouses the ethical aspirations of being verifiable, objective and factual. Conversely, The New Journalism witnessed the application of creative writing skills to journalistic endeavours, specifically: scene-by-scene construction; dialogue; third-person viewpoints and gesture (Wolfe 1996, 46). Tom Wolfe, an (in)famous gonzo himself, explained in his introduction to *The New Journalism* that, "In the early 1960s a curious new notion [emerged]. That it just might be possible to write journalism that would ... read like a novel. They never guessed ... that the work they would do ... as journalists, would wipe out the novel as literature's main event" (Wolfe 1996, 21–22). Wolfe's bold claim seems particularly relevant in the context of today's "post-truth" twenty-four-hour news cycle.

Closely affiliated with the countercultural revolution during the 1960s, The New Journalism signified a key moment in contemporary literary production in which (predominantly white, male, middle-class) writers might just be regarded as cool, in a comparable way to, say, musicians or artists. Condemnation from the literary and critical status quo (e.g. the *Columbia Journalism Review* and *The New York Review of Books*), who labelled the New Journalism as "this bastard form" and "para-journalism", only served to spark greater interest and compound the genre's status and appeal (Wolfe 2018).

Authenticity

As with the New Journalism, from a philosophical perspective, authenticity connotes commitment, for instance, to a particular lifestyle that doesn't necessarily conform to society's norms. In "Authenticity, Moral Values and Psychotherapy" Charles B. Guignon explains that "authenticity pertains not to *what* specific kinds of things you do, but *how* you live—it is a matter of the style of your life rather than of its concrete content" (Guignon 1998). In the context of this chapter, Kierkegaard's view that the "subjective truth" of one's lived experience and commitment is at least as crucial to faith as "objective truth" is therefore particularly relevant (Guignon 1998).

In order to live an authentic life, then, Guignon's suggestion is that the two parts of one's lived experience should complement rather than contradict one another. For instance, if a public figure's Instagram profile depicted a "perfect" life but their lived experience was joyless, this switch from private to public could be read as signifying a split self. The sense of being endlessly available via our digital devices means that it is becoming increasingly challenging to construct and uphold boundaries between our public and private spaces and selves. The medium favours prolific velocity, in which the speed and supply of our responses and engagement affect how our identity is performed and ranked. Heidegger's notion of authenticity puts into question both the binary opposition implicit in the process of living a double life that embraces two distinct iterations of the self but also the superficiality of quickfire digital engagement, foregrounding as it does the kind of sloganeering and self-promotion that is at odds with in-depth engagement, informed commitment and, therefore, authenticity (in its philosophical sense).

STONER

Everything about John Williams' novel *Stoner* seems at odds with the demands of this fast-paced digital-first world. In the context of this chapter, its relevance lies in the contrast between the theme and appeal of the novel and the focus and intensity of the marketing campaign, which transformed its cultural and economic capital—and its legacy. Originally published by Viking Press in 1965 without fanfare, the novel only sold around 2000 copies (Almond 2014). But when *Stoner* was reissued in the UK, after becoming a slow-burning international bestseller, its resurrection seemed symbolic. The metanarrative of posthumous publishing success functioned as a form of vindication and validation for the anti-hero, Stoner, who was previously overlooked, in a comparable way to the novel itself.[2]

The story of a young man from an impoverished farming background who begins a university degree in agriculture only to be seduced by literature, *Stoner* is an American realist portrayal of an existence of fleeting happiness and residual disappointments. Stoner's life is characterised by existential angst, as he struggles, for instance, in the face of an accusation of plagiarism at the university where he works and walks away from a brief love affair with a student. His yearning for authenticity finds a conduit in literature, which constitutes both a vocation and a distraction from the sustained difficulties he encounters daily. This is evident in his first transcendent encounter with Shakespeare in a literature class:

> William Stoner realized that for several moments he had been holding his breath … Light slanted from the windows and settled upon the faces of his fellow students, so that the illumination seemed to come from within them and go out against a dimness … he thought he could feel the blood flowing invisibly through the tiny veins and arteries, throbbing delicately. (Williams 2012, 11–12)

Stoner's response to literature is synaesthetic in its range and transformative in its affect. It alters the course of his life, prompting him to switch from his studies in agriculture to literature, which then becomes the basis of his career. In this richly redolent description, Stoner appears to be, well,

---

[2] Though as leading feminist Elaine Showalter points out, Stoner and Williams lived very different lives, with the author having been married four times and being a "hard drinker" (Showalter 2015).

stoned. His senses appear to be extraordinarily attuned to their setting as his world slows down in response to sonnet 73.

The extract above marks a shift in Stoner's status, in that his Wordsworthian "spot in time" marks an ascent, in terms of accruing the cultural capital necessary to operate within the microcosmic world of academia. Cultural capital is acquired both within the text and on publication, since the novel's reissue in association with *The Great Gatsby* exalted *Stoner's* status. With an introduction by Irish novelist John McGahern, the *New York Review of Books* edition became a Vintage Classics edition and was included for free with purchases of *The Great Gatsby* audiobook. This convergent digital approach to promoting the reissue, combined with the novel being translated and championed by the French writer Anna Gavalda, elevated its status from midlist fodder to unsung genius (Kreider 2013).

My Struggle

Exposure, authenticity and subjectivity are themes which connect Stoner's self-effacing narrative with Karl Ove Knausgård's more recent project of self-reflexive analysis, as detailed in his series of autobiographical novels. At odds with the manifest urgency of online stories and Insta poetry, *My Struggle* is a redemptive narrative that defied publishing norms on publication. A benchmark of psychological interiority, the narrator's brutal self-exposure emerges through so much comprehensive detailing of mundane domestic activity, which avoids the kind of melodramatic flourishes that often accompany memoirs of shame and loss. The detailed accounts of ordinary life seem to invite the reader to hold their nerve, to slow down and step away from digital distractedness. Indeed, this flattening of events and experiences has led some to dismiss Knausgård's work as dull, with Spanish novelist Javier Marías admitting, "I gave up on Karl Ove Knausgård after 300 pages" (Marías 2018).[3] Pushing through Ove's deliberate narrative monotony requires commitment on the part of the reader and is in stark contrast to the reading experience of consuming conventional

---

[3] "Flattening" is a word frequently used to describe Knausgård's writing, for example, in The *Times Literary Supplement*, The *London Review of Books*, The *Post and Courier*, The *LA Review of Books*.

redemption narratives, which tend to conform to more traditional narrative arcs and outcomes.

The narrator's integrity brings us back to Guignon's philosophical understanding of authenticity as being "a matter of the style of your life rather than its concrete content" (Guignon 1998). It seems authentic to the reader because what has been revealed is so delicate and obscene, for instance, the scene in which Knausgård and his brother clear out their deceased alcoholic father's home in book one, *A Death in The Family*, and the scene at his father's wedding to his second wife in book four, *Dancing in The Dark*:

> As always, alcohol gave me a strong sense of freedom and happiness, it lifted me onto a wave, inside it everything was good, and to prevent it from ever ending, my only real fear, I had to keep drinking more ... I barely registered the presence of the others, no longer heard what they said, their faces were blurred, their voices a low rustle as though I was surrounded by faintly human-like trees and bushes in a forest somewhere, not in a restaurant in Kristiansand on my father's wedding day. (Knausgård 2015)

Steeped in the heady recollections of a teenage self, Knausgård's immersive escapism is reminiscent of William Stoner's response to Shakespeare in John Williams' novel *Stoner* (2012). The descriptions are sensory and immersive, and the mixed metaphor of being separate from the wedding group, at once ensconced in a wave and seemingly lost in a blurry forest, is compelling. As the protagonist distances himself, it becomes increasingly apparent that the dissociation he is feeling signifies a deep sense of unease at the events unfolding around him, in which he has no say. It is this lack of agency that seems to signify the protagonist's state of abstraction.

As with the surprising success of backlist titles such as *Stoner*, Knausgård's status as a bestselling author is remarkable partly because it seems to constitute more than the sum of its parts. His slow, sonorous narratives reveal a concern with the passing of time by paying exquisite attention to the details that constitute our daily lives. Reflective accounts of this kind have a particular currency in this age of distraction, which writer William Deresiewicz contextualises within a broader cultural economy of slow media, citing the Norwegian example of "slow TV", in which, for instance, "state television ... 'minute-for-minute' coverage of the seven-hour railway journey from Bergen to Oslo" garnered good ratings (Deresiewicz 2014).[4] But the success of works such as *Stoner* and *My Struggle* are the result of a critical mass of influencer interest that coalesces to produce a tipping point. These two titles appear to be outliers, but the deliberate blurring of boundaries, between the protagonist and the author, is, as Defoe showed, a tried and tested promotional strategy.

In *The Tipping Point: How Little Things Can Make a Big Difference* (2000), Malcolm Gladwell explains how author Rebecca Wells' book *Divine Secrets of the Ya-Ya Sisterhood* became a best seller in 1997, thereby exceeding the expectations of her publisher (Gladwell 2002). Gladwell explains the success of Wells' book resulted from word of mouth recommendations (mainly through reading groups). The contemporary equivalent of this snowballing of word of mouth recommendations in a digital context is the amassing of likes, shares and comments on social media, which extends and promotes a particular shared interest. Because *Stoner*'s success in the UK was partly due to the grassroots recommendation of a Waterstones Bookseller (and the resultant Waterstones Book of the Year award in 2013), it was similarly viewed as being an outlier selection, rather than a lead title written by a marketable author, being promoted by its publisher, Vintage.

In *Marketing Literature*, Claire Squires observes that there is a "hierarchy of marketability" in terms of authors, which informs decisions relating to marketing spends and so forth within trade publishing houses (Squires 2007, 37). Neither the author John Williams nor the novel *Stoner* fit the usual profile of a marketable book or author. But the underdog story may have been part of the appeal, with literary journalism about the book centring on what could be viewed as a "false" connection between the writer and his work, in which the work becomes "identified as an expression of the writer's identity. The work is read through the writer's identity" (Farkas 2018, 123).

The same can be said of *My Struggle*, which was published more than a decade after Knausgård's first novel, *Out of This World* (1998), and which marked a breakthrough moment for the author in terms of sales and critical attention. Deresiewicz expresses surprise at Knausgård's success in his

---

[4] *Stoner* was part of the inspiration behind the creation of book choice app Alexi, which aims to "free readers from 'algorithm rabbit hole'", so digital predictions that promote like-for-like reading choices, marketing and publishing possibilities, which inevitably makes the landscape of literary production and reception poorer as a whole (Kean 2016).

article "Why Has 'My Struggle' Been Anointed a Literary Masterpiece?" but alludes to a similar tipping point as that outlined above with reference to *Stoner*, in terms of the accumulation of critical acclaim online, combined with a countercultural appetite among the reading public for slow media and narratives. Deresiewicz said that vocal admirer [Zadie] "Smith sees Knausgård's attention to the world around him as a rebuke to today's distractibility. But his work is all too typical of our technology-assisted culture. The novel strikes me as a giant selfie, a 3,600-page blogologue" (Deresiewicz 2014).

LIVEBLOG

Like Karl Ove Knausgård's autobiographical novels, Megan Boyle's digital-first "live" public introspective *Liveblog* (2018) is at once painfully cool, uncomfortably revealing and could be regarded as "a giant selfie" (Deresiewicz 2014). In *How Our Lives Become Stories*, Paul John Eakin argues that "Autobiography promotes an illusion of self-determination" (Eakin cited in Borst 2010, 166). Self-determination is one of the ideals of capitalism—the notion that we can always do better, whatever our circumstances. But because autofiction, Alt Lit and fictionalised autobiography question traditional aspects of the novel such as plot and character, they can also be seen to resist some of the expectations of their genres. Alt Lit has, for instance, been described by critic and academic Kenneth Goldsmith as being "usually written in the Internet vernacular of lowercase letters, inverted punctuation, abundant typos, and bad grammar ... [using] emo-heavy, homespun language, bearing the urgency and candor of a status update" (Goldsmith 2014). The disappointment the reader might feel with the narrative reflects the authors' seeming disappointment with themselves and their lives.

Boyle's confessional style is such that her reflexive magnification of her own life, and perceived personal failings, seems to signify an attempt to pre-emptively rebuff criticism. Anti-establishment sub-genres such as Alt Lit similarly interrupt the slick narrative experience of digital communication, holding up a mirror to rather less exciting, redemptive and perfect truths and instead revealing experiences that can be dull, repetitive, slow and painful. In doing so, some works of Alt Lit creates a similar effect to Brecht's alienation technique, in that they interrupt the reader's sense of narrative coherence, stable subjectivity and facile endorsements (such as Instagram likes).

In "Megan Boyle & embarrassability" Colin Herd observes that "Boyle's writing is both intensely personal *and* detachedly monotonous" (Herd 2011). It is also at once abstract and granular, for instance, in her description of taking drugs.

> i ea–i ate, i have oxycodone, and i have xanax–i ate two milligrams of xanax, earlier, and … fifteen total oxycodone tonight, since (pause) around probably like, eight p.m. and i still. i'm having a hard time sleeping, a lot. (exhale) and … um. overall feeling … um. i was feeling pretty good, i was feeling pretty good. then the thing with, um. the person. happened. then i felt pretty bad, i've been feeling pretty bad. (Boyle 2013)

Alternating between the past ("I felt") and present perfect progressive tenses ("I've been feeling"), Boyle's account of her drug consumption and emotions signals to the reader that the author's state and sense of time are similarly unstable. The single solid event appears to be the volume and names of the drugs she's consumed. These aren't recounted in a boastful way but rather as a factual necessity, almost like counting sheep to combat the immediate problem: her inability to sleep. Boyle creates an authentic-feeling semi stream-of-consciousness story that reads as though she's tapped it out with two fingers as the drugs began to take effect. This sense of real-time digital distractedness marks a departure from the dramatic depiction of binges in a pre-social world. The following extract from James Frey's fraudulent memoir of addiction, *A Million Little Pieces*, is a case in point:

> I grab rocks, stuff the pipe, hit. I grab rocks, stuff the pipe, hit. The torch is white and the glass is pink and I feel the skin of my fingers bubbling but it doesn't bother me. I grab rocks, stuff the pipe hit. I do it until the bag is empty … I have a murderous rage and I need to kill. Kill my heart, kill my mind, kill myself. (Frey 2004, 55)

Written in the present tense, this excerpt is stylistically stark. Sentences are short and staccato, which reinforces the aggressive tenor of a sketch that culminates in a desire for oblivion. Both Boyle and Frey's accounts share a similar structure, in which drug taking is both preceded by negative thinking and precedes negative thinking. But while Frey's language is heightened and angry—"grab", "murderous", "stuff", "hit"—Boyle's language, by contrast, is understated and is written for the Internet. Although she states how she feels five times in as many lines, she shows almost total restraint in providing colour for her feelings. Frey's stylistic flourishes seem overblown, perhaps exaggerated for the reader's entertainment, and his writing therefore comes across as inauthentic by comparison.[5]

AUTOFICTION ONLINE

Perhaps part of the reason that Frey's style seems spurious is because it is out of synch with what Patricia Lockwood describes as the "modes of the time", namely, "fragmentary and autofictional" writing (Wallace 2020). James Frey's public persona is deliberately performative and nihilistic, as evidenced in Decca Aitkenhead's interview with him in *The Guardian*. She describes his working environment: "He hits a key, and the computer bursts into noisy punk music—the Sex Pistols' Pretty Vacant—so loud that I can hardly hear him when he nods towards the TV and adds, 'Oh, and that would normally be on as well.'" (Aitkenhead 2011). Lockwood, by contrast, is a contemporary American writer who writes introspectively about the experience of living her life online. The appeal of Alt Lit and autofiction, in comparison to macho constructions of identity such as Frey's, is their seeming ability to represent the uneasy unconscious in a digital-first era. In her *London Review of Books* article, "The Communal Mind", Lockwood brings the idea of the Internet as collective unconscious into sharp focus. Her travels "through the internet" record the pervasive anxiety that immersion in online culture can provoke: "A few years ago, when it suddenly occurred to us that the internet was a place we could never leave, I began to keep a diary of what it felt like to be there in the days of its snowy white disintegration, which felt also like the disintegration of my own mind" (Lockwood 2019).

Lockwood's introduction is revealing, biographical and loaded. The image of being caught in a shaken-up snow globe connects with the nascent claustrophobia of the rest of the piece. This post-modern foray

---

[5] *A Million* Little Pieces recounted James Frey's experiences of drug addiction and recovery in a stream-of-consciousness style. It went on to become the number one paperback non-fiction book on Amazon.com and featured in the *New York Times* bestseller list for 15 weeks. But shortly afterwards, The Smoking Gun published an article called "A Million Little Lies" (January 2006) exposing the book as fraudulent on several counts and revealing the author to be unethical in his exaggerated portrayal of the most heart-rending, rebellious and visceral events. It is a textbook redemption story, insomuch as that the narrative begins with the author/protagonist at rock bottom in an addiction clinic and ends with his recovery.

into a dissociative state in the shift from first to third person serves at once to view and present the digital self as other and the other as fragmented and transitory:

> Why did the portal feel so private, when you only entered it when you needed to be everywhere? The amount of eavesdropping was enormous. Other people's diaries streamed around her … She lay every morning under an avalanche of details, blissed: pictures of breakfasts in Patagonia, a girl applying foundation with a hardboiled egg, a shiba inu in Japan leaping from paw to paw to greet its owner, white women's pictures of their bruises—the world pressing closer and closer, the spider web of human connection so thick it was almost a shimmering and solid silk. (Lockwood 2019)

This dense, sensory layering of images feels disparate, de-contextualising semiotic encounters with ordinary things such as eggs and dogs to create a palimpsest of signifiers that have seemingly displaced their pre-social (media) significance. Curated digital moments are captured and portrayed like absurdist momentos. The performative element of Lockwood's account here seems to mock the notion of individual agency in its allusion to the narrator as lying prostrate in a state of torpor amid the flood of omniscient content. In her encounter with the Internet, Lockwood seems to question the purpose of a remediated public sphere, in which the flattening of experiences she represents can be read as a "rejection of morality" (Burnham 2018, 88).

Clint Burnham is similarly sceptical about the Internet offering up a democratically meaningful public sphere. In *Does the Internet Have an Unconscious?*, he suggests that it is now commonplace to question the value of content shared on the Internet, which he views as being, essentially, superficial: "Twitter is just for taking pictures of your lunch—as if Stephen Shore had not demonstrated, in his magnificent color photography of the 1970s, what beautiful pictures can be made of an ordinary, fast-food restaurant, meal" (Burnham 2018, 93). Lockwood's description is reminiscent of a Stephen Shore photograph, surreal and otherworldly and yet superficial and accessible. This act and/or state of overidentification lies at the heart or rather on the sleeve of writers' intent on critiquing the cultural hegemony through a process of descriptive flattening. Everything is described in exquisite detail—bruises, breakfasts—yet overtly expressed emotion (in the work of Megan Boyle, Tao Lin and Patricia Lockwood) is largely absent. Overidentification, then, can be read as a form of disassociation, which signifies the act of disengaging from an experience that is too traumatic to process.

Conclusion

This chapter began by considering the views of several authors, in response to the apparently competing demands of expressing authenticity by constructing a public persona or living authentically by separating one's creative work from one's daily existence. It then went on to discuss the relationship between specific authors and their protagonists, and between fiction and narrative non-fiction, in order to better understand how and why certain works of literature reach a tipping point, in terms of sales and marketing. Echoing Barthes refrain in "The Death of the Author", Ferrante said that "books, once they are written, have no need of their authors" (Wood 2013). This is questionable, in the sense that the work exists in relation to the author, whether the author endlessly publishes online, publishes under a pseudonym or inadvertently symbolises (and capitalises on) a moment of cultural change.

References

Aitkenhead, Decca. 2011. James Frey: I Always Wanted to Be the Outlaw. *The Guardian*, April 19. https://www.theguardian.com/books/2011/apr/19/james-frey-final-testament-bible. Accessed 20 June 2019.

Almond, Steve. 2014. You Should Seriously Read Stoner Right Now. *The New York Times*, May 9. http://www.nytimes.com/2014/05/11/magazine/you-should-seriously-read-stoner-right-now.html?_r=009/05/14.   Accessed 17 Aug 2014.

Borst, Allan G. 2010. Managing the Crisis: James Frey's *A Million Little Pieces* and the Addict-Subject Confession. *Cultural Critique* 75: 148–176. http://www.jstor.org/stable/40800645.

Boyle, Megan. 2013. Transcription of Video Update, August 1. https://beethoventhemovie.tumblr.com/. Accessed 20 June 2019.

———. 2018. *Liveblog*. New York: Tyrant Books.

Burnham, Clint. 2018. *Does the Internet Have an Unconscious? Slavoj Žižek and Digital Culture*. London: Bloomsbury Academic.

Deresiewicz, William. 2014. Why Has "My Struggle" Been Anointed a Literary Masterpiece? *The Nation*, May 13. https://www.thenation.com/article/archive/why-has-my-struggle-been-anointed-literary-masterpiece/. Accessed 20 June 2020.

Farkas, Zita. 2018. The Role of Jeanette Winterson's Sexual Identity in the Academic Reception of Her Work. In *Identity and Form in Contemporary Literature*, ed. Ana María Sánchez-Arce. Abingdon: Routledge.

Ferri, Sandro Sandra. 2015. Elena Ferrante, Art of Fiction No. 228. Issue 212. *Paris Review*. https://www.theparisreview.org/interviews/6370/art-of-fiction-no-228-elena-ferrante. Accessed 20 June 2020.

Flanagan, Liz. 2019. This quote is from an online survey I ran between January and March 2019 (See Appendix).

Frey, James. 2004. *A Million Little Pieces*. London: John Murray.

Gladwell, Malcolm. 2002. *The Tipping Point: How Little Things Can Make a Big Difference*. London: Abacus.

Goldsmith, Kenneth. 2014. If Walt Whitman Vlogged. *The New Yorker*, May 7. https://www.newyorker.com/books/page-turner/if-walt-whitman-vlogged. Accessed 5 June 2019.

Guignon, Charles B. 1998. Existentialism. *The Routledge Encyclopedia of Philosophy*. https://doi.org/10.4324/9780415249126-N020-1. https://www.rep.routledge.com/articles/thematic/existentialism/v-1. Accessed 5 June 2019.

Harrington, Walt. 2003. What Journalism Can Offer Ethnography. *Qualitative Inquiry* 9: 90–105. https://doi.org/10.1177/1077800402239342.

Herd, Colin. 2011. Megan Boyle & Embarrassability. *3: AM Magazine*, November 11. https://www.3ammagazine.com/3am/megan-boyle-embarrassability/. Accessed 20 June 2019.

Kean, Danuta. 2016. Book-Choice App Alexi Aims to Free Readers from 'Algorithm Rabbit Hole'. *The Guardian*, December 6.

Knausgård, Karl Ove. 2015. After the Party. *The New Yorker*, March 31. https://www.newyorker.com/books/page-turner/after-the-party. Accessed 20 June 2020.

Kreider, Tim. 2013. The Greatest American Novel You've Never Heard Of. *The New Yorker*, October 20. http://www.newyorker.com/books/page-turner/the-greatest-american-novel-youve-never-heard-of. Accessed 19 June 2020.

Lockwood, Patricia. 2019. The Communal Mind: Patricia Lockwood Travels Through the Internet. *London Review of Books*, February 21. 41 (4): 11–14.

Marías, Javier. 2018. Books that Made Me. *The Guardian*, October 12. https://www.theguardian.com/books/2018/oct/12/javier-marias-books-that-made-me-Knausgård. Accessed 5 June 2019.

Mullan, John. 2018. The rise of the novel. British Library, June 21. https://www.bl.uk/restoration-18th-century-literature/articles/the-rise-of-the-novel. Accessed June 16 2021.

Rentzenbrink, Cathy. 2019. This quote is from an online survey I ran between January and March 2019 (See Appendix).

Showalter, Elaine. 2015. Classic 'Stoner'? Not so fast. *Washington Post*, November 2. https://www.washingtonpost.com/entertainment/books/classic-stoner-

not-so-fast/2015/11/02/9f0ed5aa-7db3-11e5-b575-d8dcfedb4ea1_story.
html. Accessed 20 May 2021.

Singer, J.B. 2008. Five Ws and an H: Digital Challenges in Newspaper Newsrooms and Boardrooms. *International Journal on Media Management* 10 (3): 122–129.

Underwood, Jack. 2019. This Quote Is from an Online Survey I Ran Between January and March 2019 (see Appendix).

Wallace, David. 2020. Patricia Lockwood on the Extremely Online. *New Yorker*, November 23. https://www.newyorker.com/books/this-week-in-fiction/patricia-lockwood-11-30-20. Accessed 30 Nov 2020.

Williams, John. 2012. *Stoner*. London: Vintage.

Wolfe, Tom. 1996. *The New Journalism*. London: Picador.

———. 2018. Why They Aren't Writing the Great American Novel Anymore. A Treatise on the Varieties of Realistic Experience. *Esquire*, May 15. https://www.esquire.com/lifestyle/money/a20703846/tom-wolfe-new-jounalism-american-novel-essay/. Accessed 6 June 2019.

Wood, James. 2013. Women on the Verge: The Fiction of Elena Ferrante. *New Yorker*, January 21. https://www.newyorker.com/magazine/2013/01/21/women-on-the-verge

CHAPTER 8

Materiality and Post-Digital Storytelling

I don't read books in any other way but physically but that's for my own sanity—I work at a screen all day, why would I want to read at one? (Hanna Jameson 2019)[1]

From the 1910s through the 1960s, many patients at the Willard Asylum for the Chronic Insane left suitcases behind when they passed away, with nobody to claim them. When the centre closed in 1995, the New York State Museum, and former Willard staffers, preserved these suitcases within the museum's permanent collection (Zuger 2008). The suitcases were filled with objects such as black and white photos, silver spoons, spools and clocks. Framed by the suitcases, these objects looked very much like memento mori. Translated from the Latin, memento mori means "remember you must die". The phrase has found form as a motif and source of inspiration for artists such as Pablo Picasso and novelists such as Muriel Spark. In art, a very particular set of references and conventions come into play in the representation of the idea of memento mori. A memento mori painting might consist of a portrait with a skull, but other symbols include hour glasses or clocks, extinguished or guttering candles,

---

[1] This quote is from an online survey I ran between January and March 2019 (see Appendix).

© The Author(s), under exclusive license to Springer Nature Switzerland AG 2021
A. Kiernan, *Writing Cultures and Literary Media*, New Directions in Book History, https://doi.org/10.1007/978-3-030-75081-7_8

fruit and flowers. An example of this is Picasso's "Goat's skull, bottle and candle" (1952).

The appeal of materiality underpins ethnographer Janet Hoskins' suggestion in "Agency, biography and objects" that "In certain contexts, people can seem to take on the attributes of things and things can seem to act almost as persons". She adds that "Within this framework, things can be said to have biographies" (Hoskins 2006, 74). The attribution of literary characteristics to non-literary object-texts is a counterpoint to the erosion of the physical text in a digital age, if we recognise the view that books are organic, embodied inventions, which the corporeal format itself (complete with leaves and spines) supports.

Both the asylum suitcases and memento mori are examples of object stories that symbolise loss. Biographies in this sense tell two stories, and discourse analysis is aligned equally with the words on the page and the material artefact, which offers an alternate aesthetic account. Notes, lists, embroidery, epitaphs—each of these are, in a sense, organic, material texts as much as books are. Hoskins suggests that:

> Object biographies ... begin with ethnographic research, and ... try to render a narrative of how certain objects are perceived by the persons that they are linked to, and efforts to 'interrogate objects themselves' which begin with historical or archaeological research, and try to make mute objects 'speak' by placing them in a historical context, linking them to written sources such as diaries, store inventories, trade records, etc. (Hoskins 2006)

Hoskins identifies a relationship between material production and social disruption, in which the physical manifestation of dissent serves as an ethnographic signifier of self as an expression of identity outside of mainstream political ideology. The suggestion here is that by reframing narratives, we may be able to disrupt the usual process of signification. Hoskins refers to Igor Kopytoff's essay "The cultural biography of things", in which he asks of objects: "Who makes it? In what conditions? From what materials? For what purpose? What are the recognized stages of development? How does it move from hand to hand? What other contexts and uses can it have?" Hoskins concludes by saying that it encourages researchers to ask of objects what they would ask of people. But the broader question within the context of this chapter follows on from Kopytoff's suggestion that the conditions of production and reception, understood as a physical encounter ("from hand to hand"), are a contributing factor in understanding the radical potential for the text in a post-digital age (Kopytoff cited in Hoskins 2006, 74).

Drawing on insights from cross-disciplinary case studies, from small press editions and artefacts to passion-project publishing, this chapter explores the relationship between people and the stories they tell and between ethnography and post-digital writing culture. This is, in a sense, the antidote chapter—a place in which to consider counterpoints to seemingly inevitable digital outcomes by exploring outlier examples of writing culture that stir passion among collectors and producers alike, in order to reevaluate what it means to innovate in a (post) digital age.

POST-DIGITAL WRITING CULTURE

In "Orality and literacy; the technologizing of the word (Print, space and closure)", Walter J. Ong says that "Print encourages a sense of closure, a sense that what is found in the text has been finalized, has reached a state of completion" (Ong 1982, 132). Although Ong wrote in a pre-Internet era, his ideas seem particularly relevant today, because the Internet is seemingly infinite and within that context, narrative closure becomes conceptually problematic. Ong suggests that print can offer an alternative: "Print culture gave birth to the romantic notions of 'originality' and 'creativity', which set apart an individual work from other works even more, seeing its origins and meaning as independent of outside influence, at least ideally" (Ong 1982, 133). This may be why post-digital culture holds such appeal, since it is seemingly stable within space and time, in contrast to the constant flicker of digital distractions, that "noisy informational load, disrupted by notifications" (Barrios O'Neill 2020).

In "What is 'post-digital'?", writer and artist Florian Cramer explains that post-digital culture is concerned with addressing this sense of alienation by focusing on what it is to be human, with particular reference to our rapidly changing relationship with information technology. Cramer suggests that the Fluxus movement of the 1960s, in which artist's books were produced to be "auratic, collectible objects", resembles post-digital culture today (Cramer 2012). He goes on to say that we are at a similar historical point, "where electronic books [...] are eclipsing print" which has resulted in a renaissance of artist bookmaking which "emphasises, if not fetishizes, the analog, tangible, material qualities of the paper object" (Cramer 2012).

Technological determinists understandably reject this kind of romantic attachment to material objects, with critics such as Sherman Young suggesting that books are merely "containers" for writing and ideas: "Booklovers defend the book as if the object and its contents are inseparable; as if the nature of the printed codex is the only thing that makes its contents possible" (Young 2015). Digital publishing affords consumers advantages, in terms of convenience, but one might suggest that the cost comparison should not be viewed in terms of economic capital alone. According to *Publishers Weekly*, limited edition publishing exists within a sort of economic microclimate: "Many attribute the readiness to pay high prices not simply to deep pockets but to a newfound appreciation for print, an aftereffect of so much reading being transferred to a digital space, where books are abstracted and have no material value" (Miller 2013). It could be inferred that the current interest in books as objects, and in the narratives of things, is intricately bound up with the demands made on our attention in terms of digital communication.

Paper Objects

The idea of fetishising "paper objects" has a rich cultural heritage, which Ong alludes to in his suggestion that "print created a new sense of the private ownership of words" (Ong 1982, 131). In "Unpacking my library", Frankfurt School theorist Walter Benjamin extols the pleasures of the collector and suggests that the collector shouldn't be expected to read every book they own (Benjamin 1968). Broadly speaking, Benjamin is less interested in books in terms of their "usefulness to a writer" here but is instead "concerned with ... giving you some insight into the relationship of a book collector to his possessions ... [the collector] studies and loves them [objects/books] as the scene, the stage, of their fate" (Benjamin 1968, 59–60). The rhetorical intimacy of this account achieves a state of anthropomorphic transformation when Benjamin, in a dubious analogy by today's standards, compares a book to a rescued slave girl or lover:

> One of the finest memories of a collector is the moment when he rescued a book to which he might never have given a thought, much less a wishful look, because he found it lonely and abandoned on the market place and bought it to give it its freedom—the way the prince bought a beautiful slave girl in *The Arabian Nights*. (Benjamin 1968, 64)

The emotive language used here—"rescued", "wishful", "lonely and abandoned", "freedom"—evokes a relationship between collector and object that offers insights into the cultural biography of objects and an enhanced understanding of fiction as a signifier of cultural capital. Benjamin's romantic, objectifying (in both senses) language in "Unpacking my library" (first published in 1934) seems to convey a similar commitment to the political through the personal, which is further developed in "The Work of Art in the Age of Mechanical Reproduction" (first published in 1936). In the latter work, Benjamin argued for a connection between changes in the technology of culture and changes in consciousness (Rivkin and Ryan 2004), while in the former he alludes to the "aura" of the book (Benjamin 1968). In *The Work of Art*, Benjamin returns to his preoccupation with the art of pre-mechanical production, speaking of "the quality of its presence", particularly in the context of book making:

> During the Middle Ages engraving and etching were added to the woodcut; at the beginning of the nineteenth century lithography made its appearance … Even the most perfect reproduction of a work of art is lacking in one element: its presence in time and space, its unique existence at the place where it happens to be … the presence of the original is the prerequisite to the concept of authenticity … the whole sphere of authenticity is outside technical—and, of course, not only technical—reproducibility. (Rivkin and Ryan 2004, 1235)

The quality of presence alluded to above can be read as being integral to the appeal of slow living and, specifically, slow books. Rivkin and Ryan represent resistance to reproducibility in relation to technological determinism, which Matt Tierney similarly alludes to in *What Lies Between: Void Aesthetics and Postwar Post-Politics*: "Void aesthetics capitalized on a different definition of medium when it mobilized art's world making energy—against technocracy and consensus and on behalf of collective life" (Tierney 2014, 6–7). Tierney's suggestion—that technological determinism is a reductionist theory—is symptomatic of an emerging state of uncertainty, in response to the increasing influence of digital developments (e.g. surveillance capitalism) on social structures and cultural values. Understood in this way, Tierney's suggestion that medium can be mobilised against technocratic consensus hints at the notion of the text as playing a role in the reimagining of "collective life".

SLOW BOOKS

In "The concept of cultural translation in British social anthropology", Talal Asad writes about the shift in definitions of culture in relation to E. B. Tylor's assertion that "Culture or Civilization, taken in its wide ethnographic sense, is that complex whole which includes knowledge, belief, art, morals, law, custom, and any other capabilities and habits acquired by man as a member of society" to "the notion of a text—that is, into something resembling an inscribed discourse" (Asad 2010, 41). Central to Asad's definition of culture is the notion of "symbolic power", the idea that the text (or inscribed discourse) is more than the sum of its parts. Rather, it is part of a current that captures the complex flow of ideas, and which forms an evolving—and sometimes necessarily divergent and diverse—understanding of culture and identity. Symbolic power, then, is both a defining characteristic of the field and a recurring preoccupation within this book (evident in its residual concern with Pierre Bourdieu's concept of cultural capital). In *The Book Publishing Industry*, by Greco, Milliot and Wharton, the authors state that "Books are deemed to be 'special' because they allow the reader to deal intimately with a complex array of ideas and issues, from the highly charged 'beauty and truth' variety ... defenders of the 'cultural mission' theory maintain strenuously that society has an obligation, often bordering on the 'sacred,' to ensure that books are published and preserved" (Greco et al. 2014, 1). Much of the discussion in this book has centred on the relationship between cultural capital and emergent digital writing cultures, in the context of traditions of print publishing and criticism. In a post-digital age, it seems that capital can be seen to be accrued in the creation of alternatives to fast-paced consumerism.

In keeping with this view of publishing and preserving books in a way that draws attention to a constructed sense of social and cultural value is artist Katie Paterson's Future Library (2014–2114). Future Library is an installation art project incorporating unpublished books by leading literary authors:

> A forest has been planted in Norway, which will supply paper for a special anthology of books to be printed in 100 years time. Between now and then, one writer every year will contribute a text, with the writings held in trust, unread and unpublished, until the year 2114. The manuscripts will be

presented in a specially designed room in the new public library, Oslo. Writers to date include Margaret Atwood (2014), David Mitchell (2015), Sjón (2016), Elif Shafak (2017), Han Kang (2018), Karl Ove Knausgård (2019), and Ocean Vuong (2020). (Paterson 2021)

Future Library constitutes a sustainable aspirational alternative to cultural consumerism. Because we will (presumably) never be able to read the books that have been commissioned for the project, the concept *is* the text and also the paratextual narratives, such as the films, photographs and articles that accompany the announcement of each new author. The most recent contributor to the Future Library, Ocean Vuong, explains the significance of the project within the context of the attention economy: "This is an antidote, to say regardless what happens in market trends, we have a record of what humans have found valuable, the voices we were interested in, for better or worse" (Cain 2020). Danielle Barrios O'Neill writes about the significance of "literary products", in terms of their place within a sustainable future, noting that "We're attempting as a society to learn to operate more effectively within expanded temporal and spatial structures, to think holistically about the planet and more long-term about our role as 'good ancestors'" (Barrios O'Neill 2020). The sustainable element of Paterson's Future Library is further illuminated by Hoskins' explanation of biographical objects:

> In relation to space, the biographical object limits the concrete space of its owner and *sinks its roots deep into the soil*. It anchors the owner to a particular time and space … The biographical object imposes itself as the witness of the fundamental unity of its user, his or her everyday experience made into a thing. (Hoskins 2006, 78, my italics)

The Future Library was set up to do precisely that: to situate the book-object in a particular space and to construct an illusion of temporal unity through the signifying practice of setting an arbitrary end point for the project. Paterson has thereby imposed a biographical narrative that is both known (in terms of location, intention, release date) and unknown (in terms of the content and form of the author's offerings). The project's protracted publication schedule playfully invites reflection in relation to the notion of slow living.

THE LOST WORDS

Hoskins earthly concerns and Paterson's Future Library resonate with nature writer Robert Macfarlane's book, *The Lost Words* (2017). Robert Macfarlane and Jackie Morris created "a crooked almost A-to-Z from acorn to wren", which celebrated 20 common plants and creatures that had been left out of the *Oxford Junior Dictionary* in 2007, due to what algorithm's revealed to be their reduced usage (Macfarlane 2019). The story—that the language of natural history is being eroded—runs counter to the discourse—which celebrates lost language through poetry and illustration—and this tension is the hook upon which the book's thesis—and commercial success—pivots (Macfarlane 2019). The linguistic adjustments manifest in the dictionary have, according to Macfarlane, resulted in the loss of words such as dandelion and heather and the inclusion of words such as block-graph, broadband and voicemail (Macfarlane 2019). Macfarlane's poems are nuanced and sensory, characteristics which seem at odds with the mechanisms of algorithmic reductionism. Illustrated by Jackie Morris, this large-format book is a collaborative exercise in revivifying the lost words as a means of questioning the impact of technological determinism on the natural world.

In the context of book publishing, then, cultural capital can be acquired in relation to material qualities and the growth in the market for collectible print publications appears to be part of a post-digital desire for "slow publishing" and analogue culture (Cain 2017; Flatt 2017; Turkle 2017). As Sherry Turkle suggests, while we are "tethered" to our phones, we are conscious of the need to be free in our analogue lives (Turkle 2017). Similarly, with the increase of online home-working, many consumers are seeking alternative forms of consumption in their leisure time. As Barrios O'Neill puts it: "(post-)consumers are emerging who are looking for less, smaller, deeper, slower, more interesting products and services, and are willing to pay for them" (Barrios O'Neill 2020).

VISUAL EDITIONS

This omnivorous appetite for inventive literary products across formats has resulted in innovations in publishing that are both digital and post-digital. Exquisitely exploiting the space between digital and analogue, commercial and bespoke, Visual Editions has been a publisher of "beautiful looking stories" across platforms and formats since 2010. Founded by graphic designer Anna Gerber and brand consultant Britt Iversen, Visual Editions creates limited edition books which are sculptural, collectible and experimental. Editions at Play, "a free experimental place created between us and Google Creative Labs in Sydney, where everyone can explore delightful books on mobile phones powered by the magic of the internet" produces digital narratives that match their print-based innovations (Visual Editions website n.d.).

Composition No. 1, one of Visual Editions' early experiments with form, is an approximation of a book in a box, revealing an errant narrative interiority. First published in 1962, the book was viewed as an instrumental influence for B. S. Johnson's *The Unfortunates* (1969). Visual Editions' reissue is bright lemon yellow, the title and author's name are printed in red and there is floating black typed serif text cascading over the rest of the box cover. The front of the box (or cover) also features a note for the reader in red: "This book can be read in any order". On the back, the red text reads: "If the story doesn't capture you, maybe you should start again" (Uglow 2011). Inside the box there is a novel of sorts in the form of 150 unbound, unnumbered pages. Each page consists of a "self-sufficient narrative which, when 'shuffled' by the reader, forms the story" (Uglow 2011). *Composition No. 1*, then, is a novel, a collection of flash fiction and something like a "choose your own adventure" story, in which you turn to the page of your choice, rather than choosing from a range of pages. In his introduction to *Composition No. 1* Uglow says: "The physical edition of *Composition No. 1* is an object to be held, owned and loved. The digital edition is to be read, pushed, shared, discarded and reinvented" (Uglow 2011). Both, he seems to suggest, have their benefits, but the descriptive language of the former infers a more desirable intimacy. Uglow compares *Composition No. 1* to a deck of cards and contextualises the experience of "reading" it within our "age of hypertext and 'user-generated' content [where] every narrative fragmented by links, pings, mails and #fails" (Uglow 2011).

David Detrich, writing in *Innovative Fiction Magazine*, sees *Composition No. 1* partly as a metanarrative, in that one of the characters (Marianne) is shown writing at a desk, perhaps writing a novel, so that the novel seems to be about a woman writing a novel. Taken further, this idea of metanarrative could describe the immersive experience of reading the novel, since the reader experiences a sense of disorientation as a result of the lack of structure in the book, which is comparable to the experience of distracted browsing online. In this way, the freedom from conventional form that the format creates is also a source of frustration and an abstraction that situates the narrative conventions within both literature and contemporary fine art. This is echoed in Detrich's statement that "*Composition No. 1* is a novel that is based on an abstract painting, and is itself an abstraction of the novel form with a non-linear structure, that the reader may create as a form of *bricolage*" (Detrich 2011).

Bricolage can be understood as a form of homage in that it involves repurposing existing texts in news ways. Safran Foer was so inspired by the novel *The Street of Crocodiles* (1992) by Bruno Schulz that he carved a new narrative out of Schulz's text, cutting out words to create his concrete poetry remix: *Tree of Codes* (2010). Olafur Eliasson commented that "In our world of screens, he welds narrative, materiality, and our reading experience into a book that remembers that it actually has a body" (Eliasson 2010). Eliasson's reference to the body is incisive, since Visual Editions' experiments with form seem to circulate around the body of the text. Their print-based experiments with design, for instance, are informed by a sense of absence—of pages, space, spines and so forth. The language of traditional printing processes is similarly structured around the idea of presence and absence:

> Blind embossing is like a piece of fine sculpture … An embossed image is formed using male and female moulds. Under extreme pressure, these two mould the paper to their shape, creating a multi-dimensional impression. When embossed, the image is raised; when debossed, the image is below the paper surface. (Baddeley Brothers n.d.)

Gendering the process of embossing through this printing lexicon posits the female as empty space and the male as the paper being pushed into that space, which links back to the dual articulation of architectural "negative space". This notion of a lack, which is manifested through the process of die-cut printing, is reminiscent of contemporary British artist Rachel Whiteread's work, and specifically "House" (1993) and "untitled" (paperbacks) (1997). Whiteread's works reference domestic objects as metaphors for unheard (often female) voices and the space that objects do not inhabit as negative space. In "House", she created a cast of a house in East London that was designated for destruction (Farago 2018). "Untitled" (paperbacks) is a cast of the inside of library bookcases, "a room filled with the spectral marks of books whose contents and titles appear to be lost" (Moma 2019).

TEXT AND ABSENCE

Helene Pertl's book *The Case* is another case in point (sic.). The story of a woman falling apart emotionally, Pertl, who illustrated and wrote the book, designed it so that it would disintegrate over time, through the use of "unstable binding" (a loosening thread around the book's middle). As Stephanie Black points out in "Rear view mirror": "[*The Case* is] a quietly violent book, a catastrophe made poetic" (Black 2012). Such experiments with form are part of a counter-canon that Ong alludes to in his discussion of the importance of typography for concrete poetry: "E. E. Cummings's untitled Poem No. 276 (1968) about the grasshopper disintegrates the words of its texts and scatters them unevenly about the page until at last letters come together in the final word 'grasshopper'" (Ong 1982, 130).

Novelist Orhan Pamuk's Museum of Innocence in Istanbul similarly attests to the appeal of embodied narrative addendums stemming from fictional story worlds. The museum includes a physical manifestation of the main characters from the novel of the same name. One exhibit, for instance, is a large framed scale display of 4213 stubbed out cigarettes, which represents those collected by Kemal, the protagonist in the novel, and smoked by Fusum, the young woman he loved (Pamuk 2014). Curated as a repetitive uniform pattern, the butts are at once confessional and bleak and in this way reenact the physicality of loss—the desire and the lack—manifest in the novel. Such works engage with a tradition of confessional artwork which includes contemporary artist Tracey Emin's tent art, titled, "Everyone I Have Ever Slept With 1963–1995" (1995). Like Fusum's wall, Emin's work is also inscribed (but with embroidery) with the names of all the people she had slept with. The tent is an empty space; the cigarettes are burnt out and incomplete. These metaphors are manifestly melancholy and, once more, allude to both desire and the space that's left behind when desire is lost or spent.

All of these idiosyncratic art publishing projects lend themselves to psychoanalytic readings and post-psychoanalytic critique. In Lacanian terms, this might be understood as a preoccupation, even desire for, the state of being *before* an awareness of the lack becomes apparent. Slavoj Žižek's observation in *Interrogating the Real* is relevant here:

> A productive way out of this deadlock is provided by the possibility of sublimation: when one picks out an empirical, positive, object and "elevates it to the dignity of the Thing," i.e. turns it into a kind of stand-in for the

impossible Thing, one thereby remains faithful to one's desire, without getting drawn into the deadly vortex of the Thing. (Žižek 2013, 177)

Žižek's surrogate "thing" can be understood in relation to Hoskins' ethnographic assertion that "things can be said to have biographies" (Hoskins 2006, 74). Applied to the perceived tension between print and digital, it goes some way to explaining why nostalgists are preoccupied with a pre-digital ideal state of being.

Conclusion

Because we exist within the attention economy, innovation is often assumed to be digital and this has, at times, limited the conversation within publishing studies and the publishing industry to a constructed tension between digital and print. Assumptions have been made about the value of digital technology as representing the future of books. As Barrios O'Neill explains: "the innovation focus for publishing in recent decades has been on generating more and often faster informational experiences for consumers to manage [alongside] the need to generate income from reduced physical materiality" (Barrios O'Neill 2020). This view, as I have attempted to show through the examples in this chapter, is limited and limiting. Trends in consumer behaviour are beginning to reveal that there is a growing desire for experiences over products among generation z consumers. This is reflected in spending habits, as a form of self-expression that reflects a commitment to the idea that "consumption [is] a matter of ethical concern" (Francis and Hoefel 2018).

Innovators are becoming more iconoclastic and ethically motivated, which is apparent in the advanced models of blended innovation that characterise enterprises such as Future Library and Visual Editions, as discussed in this chapter.

In conclusion, it seems that innovation and convergence are indeed as much about mindset as technology, and as much about conceptual complexity as digital efficacy, and that while the future of writing culture and literary media is (largely) unwritten, it is positively alive with possibilities.

References

Asad, Talal. 2010. The Concept of Cultural Translation in British Social Anthropology. In *Writing Culture: The Poetics and Politics of Ethnography*, ed. J. Clifford. Oakland: University of California Press.

Baddeley Brothers. n.d. Blind Embossing. http://www.baddeleybrothers.com/print-techniques/blind-embossing. Accessed 13 July 2020.

Barrios O'Neill, Danielle. 2020. Post Growth Publishing: Renaissance or Reckoning? In Ben Smith, and David Sergeant, eds. Issue 3, The Lit. https://theliteraryplatform.com/stories/renaissance-or-reckoning/. Accessed 20 Feb 2021.

Benjamin, Walter. 1968. Unpacking My Library. In *Illuminations*, ed. Hannah Arendt, 59–67. Trans. Harry Zohn. New York: Schocken Books.

Black, Stephanie. 2012. Rear View Mirror. Association of Illustrators. https://theaoi.com/2012/05/28/rear-view-mirror-stephanie-black/. Accessed 17 July 2020.

Cain, Sian. 2017. Ebook Sales Continue to Fall as Younger Generations Drive Appetite for Print. *The Guardian*, March 14. https://www.theguardian.com/books/2017/mar/14/ebook-sales-continue-to-fall-nielsen-survey-uk-book-sales. Accessed 1 July 2019.

———. 2020. "You'll Have to Die to Get These Texts": Ocean Vuong's Next Manuscript to Be Unveiled in 2114. *The Guardian*, August 19. https://www.theguardian.com/books/2020/aug/19/ocean-vuong-2114-book-future-library-norway. Accessed 12 Feb 2021.

Cramer, Florian. 2012. Post-Digital Writing. *Electronic Book Review*, December 12. https://electronicbookreview.com/essay/post-digital-writing/. Accessed 1 July 2019.

Cramer F. 2015. What Is 'Post-Digital'? In *Postdigital Aesthetics*, ed. D.M. Berry and M. Dieter. London: Palgrave Macmillan. https://doi.org/10.1057/9781137437204_2

Detrich, David. 2011. Composition No. 1 by Marc Saporta. *Innovative Fiction*, January 31. http://www.innovative-fiction-magazine.com/2011/01/composition-no-.1-by-marc-saporta_31.html. Accessed 8 May 2014.

Eliasson, Olafur. 2010. *Tree of Codes Reviews*. https://2005.visual-editions.com/our-books/tree-of-codes. Accessed 17 July 2020.

Farago, Jason. 2018. Ghosts of the Past, Embalmed in White Plaster. *The New York Times*, October 4. https://www.nytimes.com/2018/10/04/arts/design/rachel-whiteread-national-gallery-of-art-review.html. Accessed 1 July 2019.

Flatt, Molly. 2017. In Praise of Slow Publishing. *Bookseller*, February 1. https://www.thebookseller.com/futurebook/we-need-slow-reading-revolution-478141. Accessed 1 July 2019.

Foer, Safran. 2010. *Tree of Codes*. London: Visual Editions.

Francis, Tracy and Hoefel, Fernanda. 2018. 'True Gen': Generation Z and its implications for companies. McKinsey & Company, November 12. https://www.mckinsey.com/industries/consumer-packaged-goods/our-insights/true-gen-generation-z-and-its-implications-for-companies. Accessed May 2020.

Greco, A.N., J. Milliot, and R.M. Wharton. 2014. *The Book Publishing Industry*. 3rd ed. New York: Routledge.

Hoskins, Janet. 2006. Agency, Biography and Objects. In *Handbook of Material Culture*, ed. Chris Tilley, Webb Keane, Susanne Kuechler, Mike Rowlands, and Patricia Spyer. London: Sage.

Jameson, Hanna. 2019. This quote is from an online survey I ran between January and March 2019 (See Appendix).

Kopytoff, Igor. 1986. The Cultural Biography of Things: Commoditization as Process. In *The Social Life of Things: Commodities in Cultural Perspective*, ed. Arjun Appadurai, 64–92. Cambridge: Cambridge University Press.

Macfarlane, Robert. 2019. View Through a Window. *Times Literary Supplement*, January 15. https://www.the-tls.co.uk/articles/public/lost-words-robert-macfarlane/. Accessed 1 July 2019.

Miller, J.H. 2013. Art Books Future Now: Art & Photography Books 2013. *Publishers Weekly*, March 24. http://www.publishersweekly.com/pw/by-topic/industry-news/bookselling/article/56501-art-books-future-now-art-photography-books-2013.html. Accessed 1 July 2019.

Moma. 2019. https://www.moma.org/collection/works/81833. Accessed 1 July 2019.

Ong, Walter J. 1982. *Orality and Literacy: The Technologizing of the Word*. London/New York: Routledge.

Pamuk, Orhan. 2014. Translated by Oklap, E. *The New York Times Style Magazine*, March 20. http://tmagazine.blogs.nytimes.com/2014/03/20/small-museums/?_php=true&_type=blogs&_r=0. Accessed 1 July 2019.

Rivkin, Julie, and Michael Ryan. 2004. *Literary Theory: An Anthology*. Oxford: Blackwell.

Saporta, Marc. 2011. *Composition No. 1*. London: Visual Editions.

Tierney, Matt. 2014. *What Lies Between: Void Aesthetics and Post-War Post Politics*. Rowman and Littlefield International.

Turkle, Sherry. 2017. *Alone Together: Why We Expect More from Technology and Less from Each Other*. New York: Basic Books.

Uglow, Tom. 2011. Introduction. In *Composition No. 1*, ed. Marc Saporta. London: Visual Editions.

Young, Sherman. 2015. *The Book Is Dead: Long Live the Book*. Montgomery: NewSouth.

Žižek, Slavoj. 2013. *Interrogating the Real*. London: A&C Black.

Zuger, Abigail. 2008. From Forgotten Luggage, Stories of Mental Illness. *The New York Times*, March 25. https://www.nytimes.com/2008/03/25/health/views/25book.html

Writing Cultures in a Digital Age Survey: Summary of Key Findings

This survey was live from January to April 2019. All respondents are published writers. The majority of respondents accessed the survey via Twitter. I also approached a number of writers directly.

As expected, many of the thirty-one respondents write across a range of forms: 50% write criticism; 20% write poetry; 50% write non-fiction and almost 57% write fiction. The respondents included award-winning, bestselling writers and critics whose work is predominantly published by trade publishers, such as HarperCollins, Random House and Penguin. Five of the respondents are publishers or former publishers. Of the poets, some are published by literary publishers, such as Faber and Carcanet, and some primarily create site-specific experimental work. Sixteen of the respondents are female and seventeen male. One of the writers did not want to be identified, in part because of the negative treatment they had previously been subjected to on social media. The indicative quotes below are anonymised but some have been cited, with permission, in the book. The responses have been organised under the thematic headings to which they most closely relate and only a selection are copied below, because of the large volume of feedback received (more than 12,000 words). Although the sample is small, the qualitative feedback was significant in its contribution to this book.

In your view, and in your experience, in what ways has writing culture changed in this (post) digital age?

"There are opportunities to be had and I like that people can bypass gatekeepers but I'm sure being an author was easier and less stressful when you couldn't google yourself and weren't encouraged to whore your opinions out on social media in the hope of snaring a few readers. Like all of modern life, technology is a good servant and a bad master. I think there is a thesis to be written in the future where someone looks at the standard of an author's book and sees them drop off when they go mad on social media for a couple of years and then get better when they quit it."

"At the risk of sounding like a old curmudgeon, I worry that the hallmarks of short-form journalism have crept into the novel, to the point where it is harder to justify (and crucially publish) anything that is unusual, hard to pigeonhole and which dares to show its hand slowly. On the plus side, digital culture and self-publishing has the potential to overturn the old male, white, posh citadels of publishing and allow previously underrepresented voices to speak directly to readers. And even writing that last line, I'm realising that—if this is the case—my opening concern might not be so important in the long run. So overall I'm optimistic."

"Research of the kind I do—topical/historical—has got a lot easier. Though I miss finding answers to my questions in the post. I never wrote a book on a typewriter, but I can say that word processing has improved since 1990 or so and that editing and writing are correspondingly more pleasurable and less cumbersome. It's hard to be sure, but I suspect publishers generally have less time for writers. And it's nice, when a book is out of print, to see people can still get it as an e-book."

"The range of texts available has broadened reading, provided a wider account of the canons, traditions and schools writing now and in the past. As a result I see more hybridity, more exchange between UK and North America, less tribalism, a sense of formalisms (plural) has challenged critical orthodoxies, and I'd say there is a more various and broad field of Poetry being read and enjoyed than, say, ten years ago."

Is there still a need for professional arts and culture journalism in the digital age?

Writers were asked to share their views on the Reuters report titled "Anyone can be a critic: Is there still a need for professional arts and culture journalism in the digital age?" Fifty percent of respondents agreed that the democratisation of culture is good, while 30% agreed that responsible criticism is being undermined and 27% agreed that criticism as a craft is under siege. Responses were largely characterised by a degree of ambivalence:

"Democratisation of culture is obviously good, particularly when it allows for a greater range of experience and of racial and class backgrounds. But I don't think this need threaten the role of the critic. It could be argued that it actually makes good (as in informed, passionate, articulate) criticism more necessary than ever; a few trusted (or at least interesting) viewpoints amid the white noise of competing voices."

"A working democracy needs both academic critical work and a lively, unfettered popular culture. The problem I see in our contemporary culture (and since the late eighteenth century), is the lack of respect and communication between the two. This gap is about power in both directions and is related to the current 'democratic deficit' we are experiencing in the west, I think."

"I feel like criticism is often published now on the basis of how many clicks it might get, rather than the nuance of the author. And I feel like a scary amount of interaction with writing is along tribal lines, rather than an honest engagement, and often has more to do with the perceived ideology of the headline than it does with the actual content. This I'd attribute largely to the shaping force of social media and algorithmic gaming by publishers."

"There is plenty of room for both professionals and amateurs, for paid and unpaid critics. We would be poorer without the professionals, but if they are under threat it is not mainly from the amateurs."

"There is a difference between 'criticism' and 'review'. Very crudely, the former is about establishing cultural value, the latter about promoting commercial value."

"I'm sceptical that 'democratisation of culture' is really taking place, but in principle would be in favour of that."

"Seeing as arts and journalism are gate-kept industries, and white straight men are—as ever—overrepresented and more favourably represented (see the infamous analysis of *LRB* reviewing for example), other people's voices being represented in those fields is good."

Do you use social media in relation to your work?

In terms of social media use, 71% of respondents reported using social media to engage with their community of followers and 61% use it to tweet about upcoming events and writing projects they are involved with. Thirteen percent of respondents don't use social media and 61% use social media to promote the work and ideas of others.

Several respondents expressed the sense that social media can have a negative impact but is a necessary aspect of being a writer, with one author stating: "I used to [use social media] but it makes me depressed". Another author said, "I'm only on Twitter—and I'd like to quit, but I find it annoyingly addictive."

"I like writing a blog, but find that Twitter lends itself to overly simple, fixed oppositions that aren't particularly useful. All of the best things I read on Twitter are links to longer articles, usually from publications first established in print. I would note that questions about digital culture tend to focus on form, often in fixed or idealised ways. The most significant development of the digital age, in my view, relates to the degree of control we (don't) have over our own information. The 'digital revolution' has been used to disenfranchise writers and thinkers in all kinds of ways and to hugely undermine individual rights of privacy and ownership which have protected democracies since the 18th century."

"Sharing work online is just a different form of publication, albeit in some cases with format and time limits which do alter the experience. For example, taking part in a Twitter chat, I've found to be intense, trying to craft engaged and relevant responses in the moment. Afterwards, I did feel vulnerable and exposed as there wasn't enough time for the usual reflection and editing processes that I usually undertake before sharing ideas. And yet, it was certainly exhilarating and enabled me to have direct contact with readers and potential readers in a new way."

Positive responses to social media use were focused on engagement with other professional writers, with one writer saying, "I've had six-way conversations about handling point-of-view with well-known writer friends". Another enthusiastically reported: "I use it to dip my face into the vast ocean of ideas and everyday narratives that are swirling around out there—it's a fecund environment, pumping out the base-ingredients of a million stories, which I'll probably never get around to writing."

Do you think publishers have given enough thought to advanced digital content?

Responses to the theme of advanced (convergent) content tended to be short and were largely characterised by uncertainty and speculation:

"The early glory years peaked in 2011. Publishers didn't give enough thought to advanced content. Audio is thrown in plus video. But no one really wanted that so a lot of these apps weren't really that successful."

"Nobody really knows where technology is heading and space is limitless, so it follows that publishers and developers have adopted the business model of throwing everything at the wall and then seeing what will stick. As a journalist, I found it variously silly and exciting and it certainly forced me out of my comfort zone, which is entirely healthy. As a consumer, though, I tend to read journalism online and literature in books. A paperback is still the best, most user-friendly piece of technology."

"I suspect that the future of digital literature will be more 'social'—communities of readers chatting in the margins, so to speak. It hasn't peaked. But the future isn't the Kindle."

How do you feel about the idea of having an author brand?

In response to the question, "How do you feel about the idea of having an author brand?", 30% of respondents agreed that, "I am uncomfortable with seeing myself as a commodity in this way", while the same percentage of respondents liked the idea of having a writing persona. This question produced the most self-referencing, impassioned and lengthy responses, with 23% of respondents agreeing that having an author brand is "a necessary evil".

"Some years ago, I was introduced to another journalist at some party or other and the first thing he said to me was, "Good brand" and it almost brought me out in hives. Writing a novel (or a poem or an article or whatever) is hard enough as it is without worrying about whether it's securely on brand or a super-smart rebranding exercise. Just write the thing the best you can and then write something else and something else after that. The story matters more than you."

"Being published has always been about 'creating the name of the author' although it's more complex than ever in a digital age. It's going to happen, it's part of the publishing process. Even anonymous authors, by choosing not to share their 'real' identity, are creating a persona. So, I feel I may as well embrace it and contribute to the creation of the author brand, on a book by book basis."

"Depends on what you mean by "brand". I'd hate my brand persona to be Persil—bland, over-advertised and only does one thing. But I don't mind being a great, big Department Store stuffed with riches for many different kinds of person … including you, dear reader."

"On one hand: shrinking myself to something digestible and marketable is vile, and shapes my output to fit market forces—which is hideous. On the other: my persona is a buffer between my interior and the market. It lets me stay healthy, sure in the knowledge that who I am and what I sent (sic.) are different things."

"The brand is in a sense a further text, as much as the author is also in a constant process of authoring themselves. The subject as author isn't any kind of stable origin point to authenticate or tether their work or presence on social media as an extension of that work. So??? (sic.) A brand is gross but also it's a reductive term for the complexity of the situation."

"I think Hilary Mantel said somewhere that 'self-consciousness is death to the writer'. The challenge for any artist is to move beyond the self (with all its crafty censoring strategies and personal inhibitions). To have—or I suppose actually the verb is to exist as—a "brand" is surely the opposite; it is to categorise, and to limit experimentation and development by tying an artist to a specific image or version of themselves and their work. I can't see how that can be helpful to any artist."

How do you engage with writing—digital/print/audio/other?

In response to the question, "How do you engage with writing?", without exception, all of the writers surveyed expressed a preference for reading printed books. This is partly for practical reasons. As one respondent noted, most writers work on screens all day. But it may also be to do with how people feel about digital and the unease resulting from how digital data is monitored and managed. While some embraced different ways of consuming words, "I consider TV and film to be cultural texts—so I read them via video and webstream", most emphasised the importance of a book's physicality.

- 100% of respondents said that they read books made out of paper.
- 55% said that they read online and 55% listen to podcasts.
- 41% use a Kindle and 41% listen to Audible (both of which are owned by Amazon).

"Most digital frills get in the way—I prefer simply to read."

"I don't really read books in any other way but physically but that's for my own sanity—I work at a screen all day, why would I want to read at one."

Some authors emphasised the value judgments that are at play when choosing a format with some texts more worthy of a physical form than others:

"My e-reader is a Kobo. I use it for holiday reading and for books I want to read but don't necessarily want to own."

"Audible is my guilty pleasure. It's nice to be read to. But when the writing is magical I want to see it for myself."

"Everything else is just a distraction, or a projection of a third party's perception of what the narrative is about."

Conclusion

To conclude, most of the respondents acknowledged the opportunities that writing and publishing on the Internet and via social media afford them but felt a degree of discomfort about the sense of being exposed when sharing content on social media. Indeed, some expressed strong (negative) views about Instapoets and, "writers banging on like demented ego maniacs", while one writer said that "I had to unfollow a number of writers on Twitter—because while I continue to admire their writing, I found their social media persona actively objectionable."

Index[1]

[1] Note: Page numbers followed by 'n' refer to notes.